"*Re:Imagining Change* is a one-of-a-kind essential resource for everyone who is thinking big, challenging the powers-that-be and working hard to make a better world from the ground up. This innovative book provides the tools, analysis, and inspiration to help activists everywhere be more effective, creative and strategic. This handbook is like rocket fuel for your social change imagination."
~Antonia Juhasz, author of *The Tyranny of Oil: The World's Most Powerful Industry and What We Must Do To Stop It* and *The Bush Agenda: Invading the World, One Economy at a Time*

"We are surrounded and shaped by stories every day—sometimes for better, sometimes for worse. But what Doyle Canning and Patrick Reinsborough point out is a beautiful and powerful truth: that we are all storytellers too. Armed with the right narrative tools, activists can not only open the world's eyes to injustice, but feed the desire for a better world. *Re:Imagining Change* is a powerful weapon for a more democratic, creative and hopeful future."
~Raj Patel, author of *Stuffed & Starved* and *The Value of Nothing: How to Reshape Market Society and Redefine Democracy*

"Yo Organizers! Stop what you are doing for a couple hours and soak up this book! We know the importance of smart "issue framing." But *Re:Imagining Change* will move our organizing further as we connect to the powerful narrative stories and memes of our culture."
~ Chuck Collins, Institute for Policy Studies, author of *The Economic Meltdown Funnies* and other books on economic inequality

"Politics is as much about who controls meanings as it is about who holds public office and sits in office suites. Knowing how to knock on doors, organize community meetings and plan a street protest is no longer enough, today's activists need to know how to generate symbols, tell stories, and tap into popular dreams. smartMeme's *Re:Imagining Change* is THE handbook for fighting on this cultural terrain. The only problem I have with the book is that I can't keep it on my desk—all my activist friends keep borrowing it."
~Stephen Duncombe, author of *Dream: Re-Imagining Progressive Politics in an Age of Fantasy*

"*Re:Imagining Change* is worthy of praise. As an introduction to story-based strategy, the book offers organizers and advocates a new and necessary way to understand and transform the impact of stories on our public life."
~ Malkia Cyril, Director, Center for Media Justice

"Our stories are powerful enough to change the world—if you believe. SmartMeme's *Re:Imagining Change* will give you the tools and confidence to unleash the power of the stories that live in your community and make the dream of 'another world is possible,' a reality."
~Robby Rodriguez, Executive Director of the SouthWest Organizing Project and co-author of *Working Across Generations: Defining the Future of Non-profit Leadership*

"Once upon a time, left-wing activists thought being right was good enough, but the past decade has seen a more elegant and effective understanding that you need to be a lot more if you want to win. SmartMeme's guidebook to being that *more*—smarter, more engaging, more subversive, more powerful—should be in every activist's hands and imagination. It's a great toolkit for change."
~Rebecca Solnit, author of *A Paradise Built in Hell: The Extraordinary Communities that Arise in Disaster* and *Hope in the Dark: Untold Stories, Wild Possibilities*

"Brilliant and invaluable... Lakoff introduced the progressive movement to the power of framing. Canning and Reinsborough take framing to a far more powerful level and provide practical tools essential to the success of every progressive organization that seeks to bring forth a world of peace and justice. It gets my highest recommendation."
~David Korten, board chair, *YES! Magazine* and author *The Great Turning: From Empire to Earth Community* and *Agenda for a New Economy*

"*SmartMeme's Re:Imagining Change* is such an incredible resource! This is a book to consume, to go over meticulously, mark up, share with friends, and keep within arm's reach on the shelf. The format is so accessible, the analysis and case studies show how important their groundbreaking story-based strategy is for all of the work we're doing. Ruckus wants every group we work with to grab this book!"
~Adrienne Maree Brown, Executive Director, The Ruckus Society

Re:Imagining Change

How to Use Story-based Strategy to Win Campaigns, Build Movements, and Change the World

Patrick Reinsborough & Doyle Canning

PM Press

Re:Imagining Change—How to Use Story-based Strategy to Win Campaigns, Build Movements, and Change the World

Patrick Reinsborough & Doyle Canning

ISBN: 978-1-60486-197-6

Library of Congress Control Number: 2009912453

Cover and interior design by Nick Jehlen, The Action Mill

Cover image credits:
WTO banner photo: Dang Ngo http://www.dangngo.com/
Suffragettes and civil rights illustrations: Josh Kahn Russell

PM Press
PO Box 23912
Oakland, CA 94623
www.pmpress.org

Printed in the USA on recycled paper, by the Employee Owners of Thomson-Shore in Dexter, Michigan.
www.thomsonshore.com

Published in Canada by Fernwood Publishing
32 Oceanvista Lane, Black Point, Nova Scotia, B0J 1B0
and 748 Broadway Avenue, Winnipeg, MB R3G 0X3
www.fernwoodpublishing.ca

Fernwood Publishing ISBN: 9781552663936

Cataloguing data available from Library and Archives Canada

10 9 8 7 6 5 4 3

Table of Contents

Gratitude and Acknowledgements

As the poet Audre Lorde reminds us, "There are no new ideas. There are only new ways of making them felt." In that sprit we humbly offer gratitude to the giants on whose shoulders we stand, and offer a dedication to everyone everywhere who has ever dreamed of a better world and had the courage to move towards that vision.

The **story-based strategy** framework has evolved through the collective study, experimentation, and application of the *smart*Meme Strategy & Training Project in its various formations since 2002. Although this manual was written by Doyle Canning and Patrick Reinsborough, these ideas, methods, and tools have emerged from the collaboration and shared imagination of *smart*Meme collective co-founders James John Bell, Doyle Canning, J Cookson, Ilyse Hogue, and Patrick Reinsborough, as well as past and present extended-collective members Katie Joaquin, Kaitlin Nichols, Sean Witters, Kip Williams, and particularly Jen Angel who provided critical editing support for the project. We offer our gratitude to Libby Modern for her assistance and to Antonia Juhasz and Jessica Hoffman for their excellent proofreading. A special thanks to our designer Nick Jehlen for support above and beyond the call of duty and to Josh Kahn Russell for donating his artwork for the cover of the book. We also offer gratitude to our colleagues at *smart*Meme Studios, all past and present *smart*Meme Board members, STORY board members, all of the participants in the national *incite/insight* gathering, and Invoking the Pause gatherings, and other training-for-trainers events. Thank you.

We offer shout-outs to our cousin organizations and community of innovators: Jethro Heiko and Nick Jehlen at the Action Mill for applications of the "consent theory of power" in a U.S. context; Kenny Bailey and crew at the Design Studio for Social Intervention for the vision of "an imagination lab for social justice"; Andrew Boyd at AgitPop for tireless creativity and coining "meme campaigning"; Matthew Smucker and Beyond the Choir for getting us beyond the "story of the righteous few"; Cynthia Suarez for her wise words on innovation and bold ideas about the power of networks; Maryrose Dolezal and the Nonviolent Youth Collective for the application of **story-based strategy** in anti-oppression work, and the meme of "mutual mentorship"; the Movement Strategy Center for the brilliant alliance-building model and being spirit in motion; the Center for Media Justice for their articulation and application of media justice as self-determination; Movement Generation for moving the "ecological justice" meme; David Solnit for helping us go beyond "(disem)PowerPoint"; Gopal Dayaneni for pushing the points of intervention into direct action vernacular; the Ruckus Society for reminding us that actions speak louder than words; and countless communities, conversations, ideas, and people who've touched our hearts and imaginations. Thanks also to all those that have given us feedback on both the ideas and how we put them into practice, particularly Sujin Lee, Rosi Reyes, Zara Zimbardo, and Justin Francese. Thank you.

We offer respect to our elders, community of peer practitioners, and like-minded visionaries and radicals in the movement and in the academy; our 3,000+ training alumni; and the 100-some-odd social change organizations with which we have had the pleasure of partnering. We also would like to acknowledge the generous support of the Panta Rhea Foundation, the Compton Foundation, the Hull Family Foundation, the Ben & Jerry's Foundation, the Solidago Foundation, the Foundation for Global Community, and all of *smart*Meme's members and supporters who have given generously to this project. Thank you.

Finally we would like to thank our beloved friends, families, mentors, ancestors, and loved ones. Your faith and support keeps our hearts brimming with hope, curiosity, love, and gratitude.

Each one of you has taught us something—and your inspired work is the force of progress that will change our world. Thank you, and let us walk, sing, dream and struggle together! Onward!

If you want to build a ship, don't herd people together to collect wood and don't assign them tasks and work, but rather teach them to long for the endless immensity of the sea.

~ Antoine de St. Exupéry

1. Introduction:
The Power of Story

1.1 From Improvement to Innovation

We can't solve problems by using the same kind of thinking we used when we created them.
~ Albert Einstein

Re:Imagining Change is an introduction to the ideas and methods of the *smart*Meme Strategy & Training Project. We founded *smart*Meme to innovate social change strategies in response to the movement-building and messaging demands of the globalized information age. We are motivated by the social and ecological crises facing our planet and by a belief that fundamental change is not only possible, but necessary. Our mission is to apply the power of narrative to organizing, movement building, and social transformation. Our dream is a movement of movements with the power, creativity, and vision to change the world by changing the stories that shape our collective destiny.

> Movements have won public support with powerful stories like Rosa Parks' refusal to change seats, the AIDS quilt carpeting the National Mall in Washington, or the polar bear stranded in a sea of melted ice.

*Smart*Meme is dedicated to holistic social change practices—shifting from issues to values, supplementing organization building with movement building, and exploring creative new strategies for confronting systemic problems. We believe that people-powered grassroots movements, led by those who are most directly affected, are the engines of true social progress.

*Smart*Meme convenes innovators from different movements to share ideas and reconsider strategies in the timeless endeavor of social change. The heartbeat of the work—building relationships, critical thinking, action, and reflection—remains constant. But these practices evolve with new technologies, tools, and techniques. Over the course of our work, we've recognized that innovation doesn't just mean improving what is already happening; innovation requires rethinking underlying assumptions and finding the courage to re-imagine what could happen.

Innovation requires creative thinking and testing hunches with real world experiments. *Re:Imagining Change* is an introduction to our methodology and a report-back from our first seven years of experimentation in what we've come to call **story-based strategy**.

1.2 Our Approach: Story-based Strategy

> The universe is made of stories, not atoms.
> ~ Muriel Rukeyser

Stories come in all shapes and sizes: daily anecdotes, movies, fables, or pre-packaged "news" stories created by the media. The stories we tell show what we value; the deepest personal narratives we carry in our hearts and memories remind us who we are and where we come from.

Historically, the power of stories and storytelling has been at the center of social change efforts. Organizers rely on storytelling to build relationships, unite constituencies, name problems, and mobilize people. Movements have won public support with powerful stories like Rosa Parks' refusal to change seats, the AIDS quilt carpeting the National Mall in Washington, or the polar bear stranded in a sea of melted ice.

*Smart*Meme uses storytelling to integrate traditional organizing methods with messaging, **framing**, and cultural intervention. Our training curriculum explores the role of narrative in maintaining the entrenched relationships of power and privilege that define the status quo. **Story-based strategy** views social change through the lens of **narrative power** and positions storytelling at the center of social change strategy. This framework provides

Musicians and dancers from Son Del Centro in Santa Ana, California, lead a pageant of creative resistance at the 2005 Student/ Farmworker Alliance Youth Encuentro in Immokalee, Florida.

tools to craft more effective social change messages, challenge assumptions, intervene in prevailing cultural narratives, and change the stories that shape popular culture. *Re:Imagining Change* is an introduction to **story-based strategy** and outlines some of the analytical tools and practical strategies *smart*Meme has used to fuse storytelling and campaigning.

1.3 About Re:Imagining Change

Risk more than others think is safe,
Care more than others think is wise,
Dream more than others think is practical,
Expect more than others think is possible.
~ Anon

Re:Imagining Change is a stand-alone introduction to **story-based strategy** and a curriculum reader that can accompany **story-based strategy** workshops. We offer tools that can be applied to existing campaigns and explore narrative itself as a social change lens that, when used effectively, can lead to new types of strategies and action. This manual is a resource for people who want to create change and shift our society toward a more just and sustainable future.

> It is our sincere hope that Re:Imagining Change will be a conversation starter with people from all walks of life who are willing to think big, dream hard, and struggle like hell for a better world.

We caution that, like all political strategies, narrative approaches must be grounded in principles and ethics.[1] In our case this means a commitment to honesty, undoing oppression, and accountability to our partners and the communities we serve. We situate our applications of **story-based strategy** in the context of struggles for social justice, self-determination, and an ecologically sane society.[2]

The ideas and tools presented in *Re:Imagining Change* are ingredients for a **story-based strategy,** and should be applied alongside the time-tested tools of strategic nonviolence,[3] strategic communications,[4] community organizing,[5] and antiracism.[6]

This manual is divided into five primary sections. The book opens with a visual overview of the **story-based strategy** campaign model. Section II introduces the theoretical framework of **narrative power analysis**. This includes using the **elements of story** to *deconstruct* the stories we want to change as well as to *construct* the stories we want to tell. Section III presents the **battle of the story** method for creating social change narratives and messages. Section IV outlines the **points of intervention** model with a focus on action at the **point of assumption** as a means of shifting narratives. Section V presents four case studies of **story-based strategy** applied in grassroots struggles. The final section explores the unique relevance of **story-based strategy** in addressing our present political moment as defined by the unfolding ecological crisis.

We have inevitably borrowed theoretical concepts from existing bodies of work. We also humbly offer some new specialized language to communicate innovations in our thinking. Our intent is not to mystify with jargon, but rather to embrace the power of naming to communicate new ideas. We have included a glossary to define key terms throughout the manual. Glossary items are marked in bold throughout the text.

At *smart*Meme, we approach this work with a curious spirit of experimentation. After five years of developing and applying these ideas, we still have far more questions than answers. It is our sincere hope that *Re:Imagining Change* will be a conversation starter with people from all walks of life who are willing to think big, dream hard, and struggle like hell for a better world. Share your critiques, ideas, questions, and stories...join the conversation at www.smartmeme.org.

Story-based Strategy Campaign Model

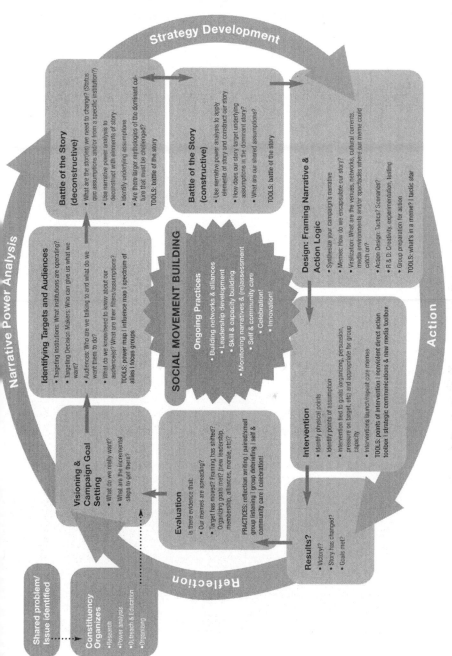

We dream in narrative, day-dream in narrative, remember, anticipate, hope, despair, believe, doubt, plan, revise, criticize, construct, gossip, learn, hate, and love by narrative.

~ Barbara Hardy

2. Narrative Power Analysis

2.1 We Are Made of Stories

There is no agony like bearing an untold story inside of you.
~ Zora Neale Hurston

We live in a world shaped by stories. Stories are the threads of our lives and the fabric of human cultures. A story can unite or divide people(s), obscure issues, or spotlight new perspectives. A story can inform or deceive, enlighten or entertain, or even do all of the above.

As humans, we are literally hardwired for narrative. Harvard University evolutionary psychologist Steven Pinker argues that stories are essential to human learning and building relationships in social groups. There is growing consensus in the scientific community that the neurological roots of both storytelling and enjoyment of stories are tied to our social cognition.[1]

In one widely cited 1944 experiment, psychologists Fritz Heider and Mary-Ann Simmel showed subjects "an animation of a pair of triangles and a circle moving around a square," and asked what was happening. The subjects' responses (e.g. "The circle is chasing the triangles.") revealed how they mapped a narrative onto the shapes. Numerous subsequent studies have reiterated how humans, as social creatures, see stories everywhere.[2]

Just as our bodies are made of blood and flesh, our identities are made of narratives.

Just as we tell ourselves stories about the world we live in, stories also tell us how to live. A myth is "a traditional story accepted as history that serves to explain the worldview of a people."[3] Myths may be mistakenly dismissed as folktales from long ago, but even today a sea of stories tell us who we are, what to do, and what to believe.

People use stories to process the information we encounter from our families and upbringing, educational institutions, religious and cultural institutions, the media, our peers and community. We remember our lived experiences by converting them to narratives and integrating them into our personal and collective web of stories. Just as our bodies are made of blood and flesh, our identities are made of narratives.

2.2 Narrative Power Analysis

Those who do not have power over the story that dominates their lives, the power to retell it, rethink it, deconstruct it, joke about it, and change it as times change, truly are powerless, because they cannot think new thoughts.
~ Salman Rushdie

In order to make systemic social changes, **change agents** must understand the histories and institutions that underlie contemporary social systems, as well as how these histories and institutions shape culture and ways of collectively making meaning.

For example, imagine the following flashback to grade-school geography:[4]

Q: What is the definition of a continent?
A: *A large landmass surrounded by water.*
Q: And how many continents are there?
A: *Seven.*

Sound familiar?

A geographical map also provides information about the mental maps and cultural assumptions of the people who made it.

Let's take another look. With the definition "a large landmass surrounded by water," and allowing that the Americas are two separate continents, there still seems to be one continent that doesn't quite qualify. Apparently Europe as a geographical area has different rules than the rest! It is neither large nor actually surrounded by water. So who made the rules about continents and defined the orientation of the modern map? Maybe Europeans?

A map is a tool to navigate the physical world, but it is also an expression of the deeper shared mental maps a culture provides to understand the world. This is one example of how the history of European colonization continues to influence the way we collectively see. Historic power relations—the social, economic, and political forces of the past—can continue to shape how we understand the present, which in turn impacts our imagination of the future.

In order to make systemic social changes, change agents must understand the histories and institutions that underlie contemporary social systems, as well as how these histories and institutions shape culture

*Smart*Meme describes culture as a matrix of shared mental maps that define how we collectively create meaning and understand the world around us. Inevitably, popular culture is an ever-evolving, contested space of struggle, where competing voices, experiences, and perspectives fight to answer the questions: Whose maps determine what is meaningful? Whose stories are considered "true"?

REFLECTIONS: STORYTELLING

Name stories
▶ What is your full name?
▶ Why is that your name? Tell the story.

Myths
▶ Are there myths, stories, fables, or tall tales that you were told as a child? Choose one and retell the story.
▶ Where did it come from (family stories, religious texts, elders, movies, books, etc)?
▶ Are there lessons you draw from this story?
▶ How does it impact your life today?

When discussing culture, media theorist Marshall McLuhan often reminded his students, "We don't know who discovered water, but we can assume it wasn't a fish."

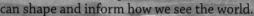

Whether you call them stories, cosmologies, myths, meta-narratives, the status quo, or some other word,[5] it is clear that powerful stories can shape and inform how we see the world. As certain ideas, practices, and worldviews become normalized over time, they form a **dominant culture** that disproportionately represents powerful institutional interests and perpetuates the stories that validate their political agendas. These stories can become invisible as they are passed from generation to generation—carrying assumptions that become "conventional wisdom."

Many of our current social and ecological problems have their roots in the silent consensus of assumptions that shape the **dominant culture:** *Humans can dominate and outsmart nature. Women are worth less than men. Racism and war are part of human nature. U.S. foreign policy benevolently spreads democracy and liberation around the world...*

To make real and lasting social change...these stories must change.

A **narrative power analysis** recognizes that humans understand the world and our role in it through stories, and thus all power relations have a narrative dimension. Likewise, many stories are imbued with power. This could be the power to explain and justify the status quo or the power to make change imaginable and urgent.

A narrative analysis of power encourages us to ask: Which stories define cultural norms? Where did these stories come from? Whose stories were ignored or erased to create these norms? What new stories can we tell to more accurately describe the world we see? And, perhaps most urgently, what are the stories that can help create the world we desire?

Narrative power analysis starts with the recognition that the currency of story is not necessarily truth, but rather meaning. In other words, we often believe in a story not necessarily because it is factually true; we accept a story as true because it connects with our values, or is relevant to our experiences in a way that is compelling.

The role of narrative in rendering meaning in our minds is what makes story a powerful force. These power dynamics operate both in terms of our individual identities—whether or not you get to determine your own story—and on the larger cultural level: Which stories are used to make meaning and shape our world? For example, which individuals, groups, or nations are portrayed as heroic—and whose story is presented as villainous, weak, or just irrelevant?

These questions show the narrative dimensions of the physical relationships of power and privilege, the unequal access to resources, and denials of self-determination that shape contemporary society. Asking these questions is key to bringing a **narrative power analysis** into social change work.

2.3 Power and Mythology

Myths which are believed in tend to become true.
~ George Orwell

Just as activists apply a power analysis to understand relations between key decision makers and relevant institutions, activists can apply a **narrative power analysis** to understand the narratives shaping an issue, campaign, or specific social context.

Narrative power analysis provides a framework to extend power analysis into **narrative space**—the intangible realm of stories, ideas, and assumptions that frame and define the situation, relationships or institutions in question.

Narrative power analysis starts with the recognition that the currency of story is not necessarily truth, but rather meaning.

Narratives can often function as a glue to hold the legitimacy of power structures in place and maintain the status quo. When working for social change, it is essential to understand specifically how these narratives operate.

For example, when confronted with ongoing injustice, some people will say, "that's just the way things are." In this **dominant culture** narrative, politicians, generals, and corporate executives have power but the rest of us don't. This is one of the most common assumptions that normalizes existing power dynamics and makes them appear unchangeable.

But **people-powered** movements around the world have shown us that *power is a relationship*; it is a malleable and dynamic relationship between those who have more power and those who have less. The "consent theory of power," popularized by Gene Sharp,[6] posits that power structures are inherently unstable and propped up by societal institutions that are operated by rulers with the tacit consent of the ruled. When the governed remove their consent or obedience from the power holders, dramatic changes can happen.

This has been the story of countless organizing campaigns and nonviolent revolutions around the world from the resistance to legalized segregation in the Southern United States to the overthrow of dictatorships in the Philippines, Czechoslovakia, Yugoslavia, and several former Soviet Republics.

Social change history can be interpreted as a struggle between collaborative power ("power-with" or "power-together") and coercive power ("power-over"). When grassroots movements mobilize and make change by uniting people to challenge the coercive power of an illegitimate and oppressive authority, this is a clear contest between collaborative power-with and coercive power-over.

It is easy to see coercive power in its most physical forms: the policeman's gun, the invading army's tanks, or the economic coercion when the boss threatens to fire anyone who supports a union drive. In many cases it is harder to see coercive power when it is operating as narrative.

In the 1930s, the imprisoned Italian Communist leader Antonio Gramsci developed the concept of **hegemony** (coming from the Greek word *hegemonia*, meaning leadership) to describe how the elite don't just physically rule society, but, more importantly, they define society's moral and intellectual leadership. Capitalism, Gramsci suggested, maintained control not just through violence and economic coercion, but also ideologically, through a hegemonic culture in which the values of the elite became the "common sense values of all."[7] The power of **hegemony** is expressed through coercion and consent rather than through armed force. This multifaceted cultural process limits the terms of the debate to make ideas that challenge the status quo almost unthinkable.

Hegemony operates in cultural stories that over time gain widespread acceptance and reinforce a dominant perspective or

Re:Imagining Change

Consent Theory of Power

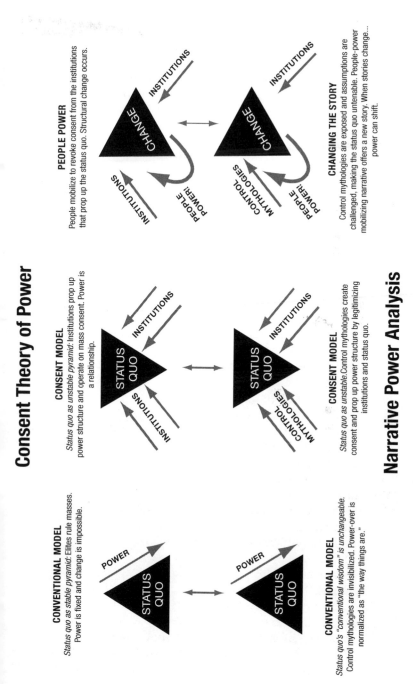

CONVENTIONAL MODEL
Status quo as stable pyramid: Elites rule masses. Power is fixed and change is impossible.

CONSENT MODEL
Status quo as unstable pyramid: Institutions prop up power structure and operate on mass consent. Power is a relationship.

PEOPLE POWER
People mobilize to revoke consent from the institutions that prop up the status quo. Structural change occurs.

CONVENTIONAL MODEL
Status quo's "conventional wisdom" is unchangeable. Control mythologies are invisibilized. Power-over is normalized as "the way things are."

CONSENT MODEL
Status quo as unstable. Control mythologies create consent and prop up power structure by legitimizing institutions and status quo.

CHANGING THE STORY
Control mythologies are exposed and assumptions are challenged, making the status quo untenable. People-power mobilizing narrative offers a new story. When stories change... power can shift.

Narrative Power Analysis

worldview. These webs of narratives are **control mythologies,** which shape a shared sense of political reality, normalize the status quo, and obscure alternative options or visions.

Referring to these stories as "mythologies" is not about whether they are true or false—again, it is about how much meaning they carry in the culture. Like religious mythologies (both ancient and contemporary), these stories are powerful in that they give people a lens for interpreting and understanding the world. Some myths evolve over time carrying harmful assumptions of hegemonic culture, while others are specifically designed to manipulate for a particular political purpose.

From the notion that "You can't fight city hall" to the idea that our economies must always "grow," **control mythologies** often operate as the boundaries of political imagination and shape the **dominant culture.** This impacts not only the political education work of social change movements, but also our own activist imaginations. By noticing and analyzing **control mythologies,** we can reeducate ourselves and re-imagine our world.

2.4 Creation Myths of the United States

Thanksgiving is the holiday of peace, the celebration of work and the simple life...
~ Ray Stannard Baker, 1919

We gave them forest-clad mountains and valleys full of game, and in return what did they give our warriors and our women? Rum, trinkets, and a grave. Where today are the Pequot? Where are the Narragansett, the Mohican, the Pokanoket, and many other once powerful tribes of our people? They have vanished before the avarice and the oppression of the White Man, as snow before a summer sun...
~ Tecumseh (Shawnee Leader), 1810

The Thanksgiving story is a snapshot of rosy relations between European colonizers and the native peoples of the Americas that emphasizes cooperation, peace, and the native peoples welcoming the Pilgrims.

However, as many of us know, that was not the reality. In fact, the first historical record of colonists celebrating a "thanksgiving" is not related to a harvest festival or to the idea of cross-

Thanksgiving is one of the most recognizable origin myths and cultural rituals of the United States. It operates as a powerful control mythology in the dominant culture.

cultural cooperation, but to a celebration of a massacre of over 700 Pequot women and children in 1637. The late-November date (which is six to eight weeks after harvest in New England) appears to commemorate the anniversary of the massacre, which was seen as a great military victory.[8]

This example reveals key aspects of a **narrative power analysis**. First, that dominant stories in the culture—ones that are widely accepted as true—are often worth examining to understand what they really say and what they leave out, as well as the underlying assumptions that allow them to operate. In this case, one underlying assumption is that Europeans were a peaceful and welcome presence in the Americas.

Second, this example shows that power shapes point of view. Clearly the story of Thanksgiving that has been passed on in the **dominant culture** is from the perspective of the Pilgrims, and not the native peoples. As the famous saying goes, "History is written by the winners."[9]

Third, the Thanksgiving story has universalized the Pilgrims' perspective as the only truth and has normalized their experience. This universalization masks the realities of the genocide of native peoples, and the mythology continues to uphold white privilege today.

And finally, the **control mythology** of Thanksgiving is both challengeable and changeable. Since 1970 Native American activists and allies have marked Thanksgiving as the "National Day of Mourning" to draw attention to the genocide of native peoples and their ongoing struggles against racism and colonization. A group called the United American Indians of New England organizes an annual demonstration at Plymouth Rock in Massachusetts. In recent years, through grassroots and legal pressure, the group has even won several commemorative plaques acknowledging the Day of Mourning and native historical figures.[10]

> Dominant stories in the culture—ones that are widely accepted as true—are often worth examining to understand what they really say and what they leave out, as well as the underlying assumptions that allow them to operate.

Thanksgiving is a central origin story of the United States, but there are many others: from "Columbus *discovered* America," to "the land of the free," "40 acres and a mule," and "Give me your tired, your poor, your huddled masses yearning to breathe free." These origin myths tell believers who we are, where we come from, and what we stand for as a country. These mythologies shape the terrain of our contemporary narratives. Understanding how these origin stories and their (often contradictory) histories impact our social change efforts today is an essential part of winning tangible victories.

REFLECTIONS: NARRATIVE POWER

Control Mythologies

▶ Is there a control mythology you once believed, but now question, challenge, or refute?

▶ When did you start to challenge the conventional story?

▶ Was there a person, incident, media piece, or experience that led you to question your existing beliefs?

▶ What lessons do you draw from this experience?

Filters

▶ Have you heard a piece of information (on the news, from a friend, etc) that you did not believe?

▶ Why didn't you? Take a moment to write down some of your own narrative filters for information.

▶ What makes you believe? Disbelieve?

Re:Imagining Change

NARRATIVE POWER ANALYSIS
▶ Examine dominant-culture stories
▶ Consider how power shapes point of view of the story
▶ Explore how the story normalizes the status quo by universalizing certain experiences and invisibilizing oppression
▶ Overcome filters: It's not what people **don't** know, but what they **do** know

2.5 Filters vs. Facts

> There's a world of difference between truth and facts. Facts can obscure the truth.
> ~ Maya Angelou

A **narrative power analysis** is not only useful for identifying and challenging **control mythologies**. It is also an important framework for **change agents** creating a strategy to reach people with a message.

Many activists spend a lot of time telling people about what's going wrong in the community and trying to persuade them to take action for change. Have you ever tried to convince people (who didn't already agree with you) about a social issue by telling them "the facts"? Did you tell them all the statistics and data about your cause, and they still didn't change their mind?

You're not alone.

It is easy to define the problem as "the general public doesn't know the facts." Oftentimes activists assume that if we could just inform people about the issue and give them the information they are lacking, then they would join our movements for change. But, in most cases, "the facts" alone are not enough to persuade; assumptions, emotions, internal narratives, and pre-existing attitudes can get in the way of the facts making sense.

Current estimates are that the average person in an urban or suburban area in the U.S. is subjected to 3,000 commercial messages daily.

A **narrative power analysis** suggests that the problem is not necessarily what people **don't** know (the facts). Rather, the problem may be what they **do** know (underlying assumptions).

In other words, people have existing stories about their world that may act as **narrative filters** to prevent them from hearing social change messages. As years of psychological study have shown us, people are conditioned to ignore information that doesn't fit into their existing framework for understanding the world (often called "confirmation bias"). These biases are deep enough that we can even track our neurological pathways of denial. As Drew Weston explains in his book, *The Political Brain:*

> When confronted with potentially troubling political information, a network of neurons becomes active that produces distress...The brain registers the conflict between data and desire and begins to search for ways to turn off the spigot of unpleasant emotion.[11]

Information that contradicts our existing beliefs is rarely able to reach through the filters of people's pre-existing assumptions. The big challenge is that these filters are frequently rooted in the **dominant culture**'s **control mythologies**.

So how does a movement challenge those assumptions and shift a story in the **dominant culture**? This question is central to developing a **story-based strategy**. A **narrative power analysis** can help us:

1. Understand the story we are trying to change.
2. Identify the underlying assumptions that allow that story to operate as truth.
3. Find the **points of intervention** in the story where we can challenge, change, and/or insert a new story.

2.6 Designer Stories and the Branded World

Advertising at its best is making people feel that without their product you're a loser.
~ Nancy Shalek

Human hardwiring for stories comes from our deepest impulses as social creatures who want to build connection in community. What does this mean in a wired, **branded**, and globalized world? Understanding **narrative power** is even more critical in the contemporary cultural context, where **advertising** and marketing have become central engines of the economy. Despite the

Re:Imagining Change

impact of the global recession Global advertising revenues are still projected to reach $450 billion in 2010.[12]

The vast majority of messages that are circulating in the mass media are created with the specific purpose of affecting the thinking, behavior, and purchasing habits of the target audience. These are designer stories created by some of the world's most talented creative minds.

The U.S. **dominant culture** is increasingly shaped by multimedia, consumer **spectacles**, and other sophisticated forms of advertising that attempt to penetrate our most personal desires and relationships. Current estimates are that the average person in an urban or suburban area in the U.S. is subjected to 3,000 commercial messages daily. Not surprisingly, recent studies have found that two-thirds of Americans feel "constantly bombarded" by ads, and nearly as many respondents felt that these ads have "little or no relevance to them."[13]

This commercialized media assault targets all consumers regardless of age. The Federal Trade Commission estimates that in the year 2004 children ages 2–11 saw about 25,600 television advertisements. This equals roughly 10,700 minutes (the equivalent of over a full week of non-stop viewing) of TV advertising a year. For comparison, adults saw approximately 52,500 ads and 22,300 minutes of advertising.[14]

Numerous studies have shown that young children are not able to distinguish between commercials and TV programs and are thus unable to recognize that commercials are trying to sell them something.[15] Other studies

Marlboro used the cowboy image and mythology to create their brand. The "Marlboro Man" campaign began in the 1950s (when filtered cigarettes were most popular with women), and succeeded in dramatically increasing Marlboro's male market share.

1931 Coca-Cola advertisement with illustration by Haddon Sundblom.

"For Santa"

have shown that children as young as age two can be influenced by **branding**, and by age three they can recognize brand logos.[16] This awareness has driven marketers to target children at increasingly young ages and use the "nag factor" to manipulate children into pressuring their parents to purchase things. Now children are literally targeted from birth by sophisticated manipulation techniques designed to create a consumer identity at the earliest possible age.

Our society has essentially submitted to a mass psychological experiment that is increasingly defining the values of **popular culture** as individualism and consumerism. Media theorist and researcher Sut Jhally has described advertising as providing "the dream life of our culture" that sells us products by selling us dreams.[17] Author Stephen Duncombe has coined the phrase "The Age of Fantasy" to describe how image and **spectacle** shape contemporary society and politics.[18]

The influence of advertising is not new, and advertising has historically played a key role in shaping U.S. **popular culture**. One example: the contemporary image of Santa Claus (the jovial white-bearded man in the red suit) is the result of a successful advertising campaign by the Coca-Cola company that began in the 1930s. The **branding** process created a dominant image of Santa clothed in Coke's red and white colors that replaced a diverse range of other depictions coming from a range of Northern European traditions.[19]

Another example is the decades old branding strategy of the De Beers diamond company. In the 1930s and 1940s, De Beers sought product placement in movies with romantic engagement scenes to popularize the offering of a diamond ring as THE engagement ritual, and to equate the desire for life partnership with the symbol of a large diamond. Within a few decades, diamond engagement rings became the norm and "diamonds are forever" became part of the cultural vernacular. This campaign is considered by the industry to be one of the most successful advertising campaigns in U.S. history.[20]

Branding operates like a magical process where a thing—usually an inanimate product, but sometimes an idea, candidate, or political agenda—is endowed with specific narrative and emotional qualities. The expression comes from the Greek and Roman penal system where criminals had markings representing their crimes burned onto their flesh.[21] Modern **branding** metaphorically burns emotional and narrative qualities into a thing so as to create in the customer (or target audience) an inseparable

How many of these branded letters do you recognize in Heidi Cody's "corporate alphabet"?[22] How many logos do you think you can recognize? Compare that to the number of non-edible plant species you can name. Or U.S. state capitals? Or perhaps the number of North American indigenous nations?

recognition. The brand is not merely a logo, color scheme, or specific flagship product. The brand is the sum total of the stories that are told about the branded entity and encompasses images, impressions, gut feelings, and associations.

Branding is one of the ways that **narrative power** is experienced, referenced, and discussed. But the popular discourse around **branding** frequently lacks a critical power analysis.

The "corporate alphabet" by artist Heidi Cody is instructive. One letter is enough to cue your mind to a specific product and possibly an entire narrative about it. Let's remember these aren't even logos—these are just snippets of the font treatments of the product names. Y is for York Peppermint Patties (and makes you feel cold like you're in the mountains), C is for Campbell's Soup ("Mmm Mmm good!") and J is for Jell-O (Bill Cosby saying, "J-E-L-L-O!").

How did these advertising images and stories get inside of our heads? How do some stories spread and saturate **popular culture** while others are ignored? This is the power of **memes**.

2.7 Memes

"Just as in the game of 'Telephone' (where a message is whispered from person to person, being slightly mis-replicated each time), selection favors the memes which are easiest to understand, to remember, and to communicate to others...Rather than debate the inherent 'truth' or lack of "truth" of an idea, memetics is largely concerned with how that idea gets itself replicated. Memetics is vital to the understanding of cults, ideologies, and marketing campaigns of all kinds, and it can help to provide immunity from dangerous information-contagions. You should be aware, for instance, that you've just been exposed to the Meta-meme, the meme about memes..."[23]
~ Glenn Grant

The concept of a **meme** is a helpful analytical tool for exploring cultural influence and the ways in which **narrative power** operates. **Memes** are self-replicating units of cultural information that spread virally from person to person and generation to generation, with a life of their own. The term **meme** rhymes with "dream." It is derived from a Greek word meaning "to imitate," and was coined by evolutionary biologist Richard Dawkins in 1976. Dawkins created the word **meme** as an analogy to the word

Memes (pronounced "meems") are units of self-replicating cultural information such as slogans (Just Do It!), iconic images that can be easily referenced (Abu Ghraib torture), catch phrases ("wardrobe malfunction"), symbols (the peace sign), or rituals (candles on a birthday cake). Memes can act as capsules for stories to spread virally through cultures.

"gene," as a way to explain how cultural practices spread. A **meme** is any unit of culture that has spread beyond its creator—buzz words, catchy melodies, fashion trends, ideas, rituals, images, and the like. Writer and memeticist Glen Grant defines **memes** as "contagious information patterns."[24]

At *smart*Meme we think of a **meme** as a capsule for a story to spread. If you want to challenge and transform the **dominant culture** and spread new ideas, you need some vocabulary to talk about the units of culture, and analyze how stories spread, stick, morph,

Re:Imagining Change

and change. **Memes** are rapidly fertilized and cross-pollinated in today's 24/7 multimedia environment. As **change agents** we need ways to track how information spreads and shapes political discourse.[25]

Memes are everywhere, from personal mannerisms and collective ritual to the advertising slogans and political jargon that dominate the media. Almost anything can be called a **meme**—but how effective a **meme** is it? Will it be a passing fad (pet rocks) or an ongoing cultural ritual (shaking hands)? Over time most **memes** tend to morph, disappear, or even dramatically change in meaning, but some prove to be resilient and shape the evolution of cultures.

> *A well-tested sound byte or powerful image alone will not win campaigns or invoke systemic change, but the right meme CAN help our organizing become exponentially more effective.*

The concept of the **meme** as an analytical tool and metaphor is useful for understanding the contemporary context of **narrative power**: information saturation, 24-hour news cycles, non-stop marketing, and sophisticated government and corporate misinformation campaigns. However, that does NOT mean that a "magic meme" will ever replace real world struggle.

A well-tested sound byte or powerful image alone will not win campaigns or invoke systemic change. But the right **meme** CAN help our organizing become exponentially more effective. The **story-based strategy** approach is not intended to be a replacement for traditional organizing and movement building, but rather a set of complementary tools made all the more relevant by the contemporary cultural context.

2.8 Control Memes

If you believe certain words, you believe their hidden arguments.
~ The Open-Ended Proof from The Panoplia Prophetica

The concept of a **meme** can make our own storytelling more powerful and viral. It can also help us analyze the stories we are working to change in the **dominant culture**.

Advertising is full of powerful designer **memes**—catchy little phrases that get endlessly repeated like Nike's swoosh and catch phrase "Just Do It!" Likewise, unscrupulous **power-holders**

A designer control meme:

Republicans put purple ink on their fingers for Bush's 2005 State of the Union Address. The purple dye invoked the ink that was applied to Iraqi citizens' fingers at the polls after they cast their vote in the first election since the U.S. invasion. For Republicans, it served as a visual cue for the Bush administration's new "Freedom is on the March" story of U.S. foreign policy. This control meme was created in an attempt to re-justify a military invasion that had been exposed as an illegal operation based on lies—when the U.S. failed to discover weapons of mass destruction in Iraq.

have shown considerable skill at designing **memes** that carry their stories through the culture: "family values," "weapons of mass destruction," "the war on terror," "the liberal media," and "tax relief" have become part of the public discussion, carrying with them the worldview and assumptions of their creators.

When a designer **meme** acts as a container for control myths, or replicates oppressive stories and spreads them throughout the **popular culture**, *smart*Meme calls it a **control meme**. A **control meme** is created (or sometimes just exploited) to insert a status

CONTROL MEMES
Some of our favorite examples:

Manifest destiny	Surgical strike
Separate but equal	Islamofascism
The war on... (communism, drugs, terror)	The liberal media
	The P.A.T.R.I.O.T. Act
Free trade	Family values
Death tax	Jobs versus the environment
Clean coal	Too big to fail
No Child Left Behind	Post-racial
Target of opportunity	

Re:Imagining Change

quo bias (or power-holders' perspective) into popular perceptions and shared cultural narratives. A **control meme** spreads a specific **framing** of an idea or situation that reinforces the status quo and/or relationships of power-over.

Some **control memes** are contemporary designer memes crafted by political spin advisors and PR flacks, such as "The Bush administration's War on Terror." Other **control memes** are the sound bites or buzzwords that mask histories of violence and oppression. For instance, "Columbus discovered America" is a neat control meme package for the story of the European colonization of the Americas. If the **meme** package for this story was "Columbus invaded America," then the story would be perceived differently.

Control meme is a name for a specific application of **narrative power** that succinctly marginalizes, co-opts, and limits the appeal of social change ideas. Many **control memes** are found in

Associated Press
Tue Aug 30,11:31 AM ET
"A young man walks through chest deep floodwater after **looting** a grocery store in New Orleans on Tuesday, Aug. 30, 2005."

AFP/Getty Images/Chris Graythen)
Tue Aug 30, 3:47 AM ET
"Two residents wade through chest-deep water after **finding** bread and soda from a local grocery store after Hurricane Katrina came through the area in New Orleans, Louisiana."

the intergenerational cultural patterns of internalized racial superiority and inferiority[26] and in the rationalizations created by the **dominant culture** to justify patterns of oppression.

In the example (previous page) of media coverage of Hurricane Katrina, white people "find" resources at a local grocery store, while a black youth is described as "looting." This is a racist **control mythology** in operation, neatly packaging an entire history of the criminalization and dehumanization of African Americans in the **meme** "loot." This particular example became an internet **meme** of its own when media justice activists highlighted it as an example of racist media coverage.

2.9 Applying Narrative Power Analysis: Elements of Story

> Truth and Power belong to those who tell a better story.
> ~ Stephen Duncombe

Telling a compelling social change story has many dimensions.[27] In order to apply a **narrative power analysis** and create effective **story-based strategies**, it is helpful to understand the key narrative elements that allow stories to operate. *Smart*Meme's model is to examine five **elements of story** that we have found are particularly relevant for both analyzing and effectively communicating stories: Conflict, Characters, Imagery, Foreshadowing, and Assumptions. Identifying these elements helps us deconstruct the stories we want to challenge and to construct the stories we want to tell.

Conflict
Conflict is the backbone of narrative. This is what defines the drama and point of view of the story and makes it interesting. The conflict frames the narrative. No conflict, no plot, no story. What does the story present as the problem? How does the framing create conflict? Who are the good guys? Who are the bad guys? What is at stake?

Characters
Good stories have characters to which people can relate. This helps people see themselves reflected in the story and choose sides. Sometimes these characters are the subjects of the story and sometimes they are the protagonists, or even narrators, and act as

messengers that deliver the story. Messengers are just as important (if not more important) as the message itself, because they embody the message. Messengers put human faces on the conflict, and put the story in context. The institutional biases of the media often present politically marginalized people as being at fault for their own problems or as helpless victims, or do not let them speak at all. The dynamics of who gets to speak, how the "sympathetic" roles are cast, and who is represented as the heroes, victims, and villains, are key to the **battle of the story**, and the struggle for self-determination and media justice.

Imagery (Show Don't Tell)

A picture is worth a thousand words. Today's mass media culture is image driven and many stories are illustrated with carefully produced visuals. Effective stories use words to create powerful imagery that captures the imagination with metaphor, anecdote, and descriptions that speak to our senses. "Show don't tell," means that the story's meaning or moral is shown to us rather than told to us. Effective stories communicate by connecting to what people already know and hold dear—our values. When a story is showing, instead of telling, it offers the audience the opportunity to use their own values to draw conclusions.

> *Identifying and challenging underlying assumptions is probably the most important element to changing a story.*

Foreshadowing

Every story has a beginning, middle, and an end—the resolution of the conflict. The literary term "foreshadowing" refers to the ways that a story provides hints to its outcome. Think of the movie that slowly pans across the gun on the wall in an early scene. We are trained by narrative conventions to perceive that image as relevant information and we know it means the gun is going to return to the plot. Real-world narratives that shape culture and politics also foreshadow. When analyzing a narrative, look at how the story suggests a specific future or makes promises (explicit or otherwise) about the resolution of the conflict.

Assumptions

Assumptions make up the glue that holds the story together; they are the unstated parts of the story that you have to accept in order to believe the narrative is true. Assumptions can take the form of shared values (a belief in democracy) or distorted information (Saddam Hussein is connected to 9/11). Often times **control myths** shape stories at the level of their unstated assumptions. Identifying and challenging underlying assumptions is probably the most important element to changing a story. Likewise, when we unearth the underlying assumptions of an activist campaign narrative, we can benefit from a shared understanding of the glue that holds the group together: our worldview and values.

REFLECTIONS: ELEMENTS OF STORY

Share a Story

Find a person willing to listen and recount a story about an embarrassing moment, a hectic morning, or a journey you've taken. You can also choose to share the origins of a personal object you have with you (like your shoes, keys, or jewelry).

Now, ask your listener to help you practice identifying the elements of story. What is the conflict? Who are the characters? What imagery was used and how was the ending foreshadowed? Are there underlying assumptions that make the story believable?

Moving Stories

Think of a story that you found moving (could be something you heard secondhand, a movie, a poem, a family story, from a book, etc.) and retell it. Why is it powerful for you? How does it use the elements of story? What are some of the underlying assumptions that resonate with you?

The problem is not changing people's consciousness but the political, economic, institutional regime of the production of truth.

~ Michel Foucault

3. Winning the Battle of the Story

3.1 The Story of the Battle

Action is the antidote to despair.
~ Joan Baez

Any communications or organizing strategy must begin with a shared understanding of goals and audience. The first step is setting goals: What do we really want? What are the incremental steps to get us there? Next, we need to understand our target(s) and audience(s) by asking ourselves: Who are we talking to? And, what do we want them to do?

The answers to these questions distinguish between two different types of social change narratives. In order to succeed in a social change effort it is essential to understand which type of story you are trying to tell. The **story of the battle** is about mobilization; the **battle of the story** is about persuasion.

In general, a large part of effective organizing is successfully mobilizing people who already agree with your cause. This involves reaching out to the audiences who already share much of your worldview and core values—they may be your base of support, allies, or a constituency with a shared experience of the social

> *In order to succeed in a social change effort it is essential to understand which type of story you are trying to tell. The story of the battle is about mobilization; the battle of the story is about persuasion.*

HUNGRY FOR JUSTICE?

www.sacmobilization.org

mobilize in sacramento
converge june 20-25 2003

This postcard uses the story of the battle to promote a mobilization against biotechnology at a global agriculture Ministerial conference. The image re-purposes the Cold War era "domino theory" meme for activists and implies that this mobilization will help topple the other dominoes. By contextualizing the action in the broader political struggles against free trade, this effort succeeded in bringing activists from the anti-war and anti-globalization movements to create the largest protest against genetic engineering in U.S. history.

problem you are confronting. This means you can tell a story that operates on some shared assumptions (corporations aren't trustworthy, human rights must be protected, the mayor is corrupt, etc).

*Smart*Meme calls this type of narrative the **story of the battle.** It can be a more literal, partisan, or tactical story about what is happening and what needs to happen. It is intentionally designed for reaching people who already share some key assumptions and worldviews but need to be activated for a specific purpose. It works most effectively with an audience who is open to seeing their own action as part of the unfolding story. Action alerts, funding appeals, progressive independent media, and stump speeches are often a rallying cry that tells the **story of the battle.**

The advertisement (following page) was created in the lead up to the invasion of Iraq to promote the newly launched United for Peace & Justice, a national clearinghouse of resources and organizing against the war. This is the story of the battle in action!

If you see it out of context, you may dismiss the message as self-marginalizing, but this advertisement was not designed for a mass audience. It ran exclusively in progressive and radical publications to target people whose views were marginalized amidst the mainstream media's pro-war hype. Everything about the ad appeals to an activist audience: the values-based message that war itself is wrong, the confrontational tone, and the declaration that the present political moment is "a time of madness." The ad's message isn't designed to persuade, but rather to mobilize

Re:Imagining Change

the existing base of anti-war people to take action.

The **story of the battle** can deepen the analysis and commitment of existing supporters and engage them in our activities. However, it often has limited appeal beyond the converted. In this example, the ad doesn't challenge the pro-war narrative. To use the old metaphor, the **story of the battle** is effective for mobilizing the choir, but it doesn't necessarily organize the congregation. That's not

Created by John Beske (johnbeske.com) in 2003.

the goal. While it is important to galvanize our movements, the **story of the battle**, is not intended to persuade the uninitiated or the broader public.

3.2 The Battle of the Story

> The destiny of the world is determined less by the battles that are lost and won than by the stories it loves and believes in.
> ~ Harold Goddard

In order to reach a larger audience, we need narratives that are rooted in persuasion. This doesn't mean telling our truth louder or more stridently; it means changing hearts and minds. Crafting a successful **story-based strategy** requires analyzing and understanding the power of storytelling to structure information in a way that convinces people who are not already actively supporting the cause.

It is important to note here that sophisticated public relations and propaganda operations often use narratives that play to stereotypes, and use iconic imagery to tell a story that makes it seem like **power-holders** speak on behalf of a story's sympathetic characters. This "power-over" model of public relations usually relies on outside experts to craft a story about the issue without accountability to the affected communities.[1]

We believe that an effective **story-based strategy** must be developed through a "power-with" partnership model that emphasizes both process and content. **Story-based strategy** amplifies the voices of impacted people telling their own story. This means the strategy is developed collectively with constituent leadership—and carried out through ongoing accountable relationships with the people and communities who are impacted and involved.

A **narrative power analysis** is designed to expose potential obstacles for a social change message connecting with an audience. Since an audience's existing stories will filter new facts or information, **change agents** need to offer a new story. Every social change effort is inherently a conflict between the status quo and the **change agents** to control the **framing** of an issue. *Smart-Meme* calls this contest the **battle of the story**.[2]

In the macro sense, the **battle of the story** is the larger struggle to determine whose stories are told, how they are framed, how widely these stories are heard, and how deeply they impact the dominant discourse. The **battle of the story** is the effort to communicate the *why*—the interpretation and relevance of actions and issues—that helps a social change message reach a broader section of the public. To succeed in changing the dominant culture's **framing** of an issue, our movements must win the **battle of the story**.

The **battle of the story** utilizes the same five **elements of story**—Conflict, Characters, Imagery, Foreshadowing, and Assumptions—to deconstruct a narrative (as explored in Section 2.9) and to construct a narrative (as we will explore here).

REFLECTIONS: STORY OF THE BATTLE

Movement Stories
▶ Share a story about a social change leader, event, victory, or defeat. Passing on these stories keeps our movements reflective and connected to our histories.

Mobilizing Stories
▶ What are some of the stories you tell to get people excited, fired up, and ready to take action?
▶ Could you hone this story using the 5 elements of story?
▶ Practice your stump speech with a friend!

WHOSE STORY?	POWER-HOLDERS /STATUS QUO Deconstructive	CHANGE AGENTS Constructive
CONFLICT How is the conflict being framed? Who is the conflict between? (X vs. Y)		
CHARACTERS Who are the victims? Villains? Heroes? Who are the messengers that tell the story?		
IMAGERY (SHOW DON'T TELL) How does the story show us (rather than tell us) what's important? How does the story engage our values and encourage us to choose sides?		
FORESHADOWING How does each story show us the future? What is the vision that the story offers for resolving the conflict?		
ASSUMPTIONS What are the underlying assumptions? What does someone have to believe to accept the story as true?		
INTERVENTION What are the other story's vulnerabilities? Limits? Contradictions? Lies? How can underlying assumptions or values be exposed? (See *Point of Intervention Worksheet*, p.79)		

3. Winning the Battle of the Story

*Smart*Meme has created a tool—the **battle of the story** worksheet—to facilitate this process. The tool, available at *smart*Meme.org, asks social change groups to examine the multiple sides (at least two) of the story they are trying to change using the five **elements of story.**

When deconstructing the **power-holder** or status quo story, the purpose of the exercise is not to explain what is true, but to tell the story *as it is told.* Oftentimes, this may involve a distorted perspective or even lies, but the goal is to understand how the story operates in order to change it. (Sometimes it helps to role-play a specific person such as the targeted **power-holder** or a company's public relations person.)

When constructing the **change agent** narrative in the **battle of the story** process, the purpose is to identify elements you are currently using, and brainstorm some new ways to tell the story. The process should be energizing for a group as new ideas come up in the exercise. Often a group will uncover new ways to frame their issue, surface the need to reach out to new groups who should be characters, explore new imagery, or gather insights on how to intervene in the dominant story. (Section IV explores interventions in depth.)

3.3 Framing the Conflict

In politics, whoever frames the debate tends to win the debate.
~ George Lakoff

Framing is a progressive buzzword, thanks in large part to the recent popularity of cognitive linguist George Lakoff's important work.[3] The roots of the modern framing discourse are in the work of Erving Goffman and his 1974 book, *Frame Analysis: An Essay on the Organization of Experience.* Goffman used the idea of frames to label "schemata of interpretation."[4] In other words, the **frame** is the larger story that shapes the understanding of information, experiences, and messages.

Framing helps define a story by setting the terms for how to understand it. Like a frame around a piece of art or the edges of the television screen, the frame focuses and organizes our perception, drawing attention to what's within it. The frame defines what is part of the story and (often more importantly) what is not, both visually and cognitively. We make meaning from what is inside the frame and we ignore what is outside of it.

Re:Imagining Change

Story-based strategy is a method for framing issues and designing campaigns. The five **elements of story** provide the scaffolding to construct a frame by offering a framework for what goes *inside* the frame.

For *smart*Meme, **framing** is more than coming up with a catchy slogan. **Framing** is the task of designing a narrative complete with characters, conflicts, images, and foreshadowing that reinforces a good story and creates meaning for an audience.

We believe **framing** is an important concept because it is fundamentally about the issue of power in the story. **Story-based strategy** explores who does and does not have power in the story, with the aim of shifting power in the story. This interplay of power and representation is the essence of **framing** and **reframing**.

When U.S. troops arrived in central Baghdad, people in the United States saw the footage of throngs of Iraqis cheering as the statue of Saddam Hussein was toppled in Baghdad's central plaza. This image spread throughout the mainstream U.S. media as a symbol of the quick and decisive success of the U.S.-led invasion. The story was about liberation—a grateful civilian population rising up to overthrow a symbol of the dictatorship of Saddam Hussein. The image gives us the impression of widespread support for the U.S. invasion. It also invokes the

Screen shot of CNN covering the arrival of U.S. troops in Baghdad's Firdos Square on April 9, 2003.

Coverage of the arrival of U.S. troops in Baghdad's Firdos Square on April 9, 2003, taken from the vantage point of the Palestine Hotel. Picture from the Reuters International News Wire.

iconic images from the end of the Cold War, as Soviet-era statues were pulled down across Russia and Eastern Europe.

> Q: So who has the power in this story?
> A: The Iraqi people, of course!

The second image is a picture of the same event, taken at almost the same time—shortly before the statue is toppled. We can see the small group gathered near the statue and 13 U.S. tanks surrounding the plaza. So, who has the power in this story?

Expanding the frame of the picture reframes the entire story and changes our understanding of who has the power.

While this is an extreme example, these two images provide a simple and effective visual definition of **framing**—you see what is inside the frame and you don't see what's outside it. When we reframe, we get a different interpretation of events. In order to change the story and change our understanding of the story's power dynamics, we often have to expand the frame or **reframe**.

Re:Imagining Change

3.4 Creating Narrative Frames

Each man should frame life so that at some future hour fact and dreaming meet.
~ Victor Hugo

So, how do movements create **frames** to shift the popular understanding of important stories and issues? Social change efforts can help shape the interpretation of important events not by manipulating the physical frame on information (as the U.S. military has in Iraq), but rather by creating a narrative frame for our audiences to see an issue. One example is a **framing** action: an action designed to influence the audience's understanding of an unfolding narrative.

Banner hung on Nov. 29, 1999, by the Ruckus Society and Rainforest Action Network in Seattle, the day before the mass protests shut down the World Trade Organization meeting.

For example, the "WTO vs. Democracy" banner was an intervention on the day before massive protests shut down the World Trade Organization meeting in 1999. The action was intended to shape media coverage in the lead-up to the mass actions. The larger frame of democracy connected the issues of labor standards, environmental protection, and human rights. By providing an overarching message that the WTO is fundamentally undemocratic, the action offered the U.S. public a frame to understand why people were protesting and how the issue could affect them. Part of why this action was so effective as a narrative framing device was that the WTO was largely unknown to the U.S. public, so activists could define many people's first impressions without having to overcome preconceptions about the WTO.

Social change campaigns aren't usually framing new issues, but rather working to reframe existing ones. This means taking on the existing stories and control myths by challenging assumptions and shifting popular perception.

3.5 Reframing

The fight is never about grapes or lettuce. It is always about people.
~ Cesar Chavez

Social change campaigns aren't usually framing new issues, but rather working to reframe existing problems. This means taking on the existing stories and control myths by challenging assumptions and shifting popular perception.

Symbols, by their nature, are powerful **memes** loaded with meaning, and can be very effective capsules for a story. Like all **memes**, the meaning of a symbol can change over time as it is reinterpreted, and the meaning of the symbol is contested. The *yellow ribbon* is a rich example of both a **control meme** and of **reframing** efforts in the U.S. anti-war movement.

A symbol created by meme capaigner Andrew Boyd and eventually adopted by Military Families Speak Out as their logo.

The yellow ribbon dates back to the U.S. Civil War as a symbol of hope that loved ones would return unharmed. During the Iran hostage crisis in 1979-81, the yellow ribbon was popularized and used as a symbol of hope for the hostages' safe return. In the first Gulf War, the meaning of the yellow ribbon began to shift to an association with the phrase "support our troops." This phrase's meaning went beyond just concern for the troops' safety to include the idea that, if you support the troops, you can't criticize the war. This is a powerful **control meme** that was used to attack the peace movement (both in 1990 and again in the lead-up to the 2003 invasion) by creating an artificial dichotomy that **frames** opponents to the invasion of Iraq as unpatriotic and unsupportive of the troops.

The yellow ribbon **control meme** frustrated many anti-war activists with its ubiquity and untouchableness. Many tried to challenge the symbol, but just writing "peace" on the same yellow loop-shaped magnet doesn't **reframe** its meaning. The yellow ribbon's interpretation as support for the war remains the overarching story.

Long-time creative activist and **meme**-maker Andrew Boyd helped launch an alternative narrative by merging the yellow ribbon with the peace symbol. Combining what had previously been opposing symbols—the anti-war peace symbol and the pro-war yellow ribbon—the conflict has been **reframed** to show that being

Re:Imagining Change

anti-war is also being pro-troops. This **reframing** challenges the **control meme** by exposing the unstated assumption that support for the troops means you can't oppose the war. The new **meme** finishes the sentiment "support the troops" with "bring them home now."

3.6 Characters

If you will practice being fictional for a while, you will understand that fictional characters are sometimes more real than people with bodies and heartbeats.
~ Richard Bach

In the **battle of the story,** the issue of who tells the story is often as important as the story itself. In the case of the peace ribbon **meme,** *who* uses it, has been key to its success. It was adopted as the logo of Military Families Speak Out,[9] an organization of people with family in the armed services who question the war.

Every social change story has lots of characters; deciding which characters should be the focus is a significant organizing and strategy question. For example, should narratives about global warming emphasize polar bears, residents of South Pacific island nations, urban youth of color who could get green energy jobs, or all of the above?

Ask: Who is impacted? Who are the victims? Villains? Heroes?

Audiences naturally look for characters we can identify with. Which characters do we sympathize with or relate to? These characters have the power to personalize the story and deepen the audience's connection.

The **battle of the story** is often the battle over who gets to speak for the sympathetic characters. Do impacted people get to speak for themselves? **Power-holders** sometimes **frame** their story by casting the very people who are negatively impacted by their plans as the characters in their story. Attacks on welfare are presented as benefiting working mothers. The timber industry uses fears about forest fires as an excuse to "protect" public forest lands by clear-cutting them. We are told corporate tax cuts are undertaken on behalf of the unemployed. After the World Trade Organization talks collapsed in Seattle, the *Economist* magazine didn't put a sulking millionaire on the cover—they featured a starving child and claimed the protests hurt the world's poor. Time and time

This advertisement for a pro-biotech industry group uses a "farmer" as a sympathetic character.

Real Vermont family farmers marching against agricultural biotechnology.

again, unscrupulous **power-holders** employ Orwellian logic to hide their agenda behind the stories of real people who are more sympathetic characters.

Farmers have been used as symbols of wholesome Americana for generations. When it comes to food and agriculture they are deeply trusted spokespeople. *Smart*Meme has supported family farmers challenging corporate control of agriculture and unregulated genetic engineering of food crops. But, as with many issues, the **battle of the story** over "who are the real farmers?" takes center stage.

The biotech industry is constantly trying to associate itself with family farmers, despite the fact that every major family farming organization in the world has come out against the industry. Advertisements produced by the biotechnology industry often feature a "farmer," but he's not a real farmer—he's an actor dressed up to look like a farmer. The real farmers are protesting with homemade banners, as in the picture to the left of family farmers leading a march with the organization Rural Vermont. But, to the average person disconnected from farming communities, which image looks more like a farmer, the iconic image from the ad, or the real farmers attending a protest?

Herein lies one of the conundrums of waging the **battle of the story** against media-savvy **power-holders** and their slick PR machines. When the impacted people are cast as characters in the **power-holder** story, the fight often becomes a contest to assert who the real impacted people are, and which side they are on. Grassroots organizing can win the **battle of the story** against multimillion-dollar

Organized by Iraq Veterans Against the War in March 2008, Winter Soldier: Iraq & Afghanistan: Eyewitness Accounts of the Occupations was four days of testimony by veterans, active-duty military service members, and civilians with firsthand knowledge of the U.S. operations in Iraq and Afghanistan.

propaganda efforts. But it requires an effective **story-based strategy** to anchor the campaign and communicate the reality of the issue.

During their so-called War on Terror, the Bush administration constantly claimed to be speaking on behalf of "the troops" and associated itself with the sympathetic character of the young patriotic soldier serving in Iraq. Iraq Veterans Against the War (IVAW)[10] offers a powerful example of the **battle of the story** amplifying the voices of those most impacted.

IVAW is led by veterans and is organizing military service members and veterans to end the occupation of Iraq, win reparations for the Iraqi people, and gain full medical benefits for all veterans. In March 2008, IVAW organized *Winter Soldier—Iraq & Afghanistan: Eyewitness Accounts of the Occupations*, four days of eyewitness testimony from veterans, aid workers, civilians, and journalists who have been in the midst of the occupations of Iraq and Afghanistan. The hearings, which were webcast and widely covered by international media, earned coverage in military publications such as *Stars & Stripes* and *Army Times*. By promoting their own boots-on-the-ground expertise about the occupations, IVAW has been a key force in **changing the story** about the war and mobilizing resistance by GI's and veterans.

Through their organizing efforts and the Winter Solider process, IVAW is emerging as a new protagonist in the anti-war story. The hearings resulted in an exponential rise in both IVAW's notoriety and membership. Their ongoing efforts are building a base in the military community, a key constituency to ending the current occupations, and hopefully preventing future wars.

3.7 Imagery: Show Don't Tell

If you tell me, it's an essay. If you show me, it's a story.
~ Barbara Green

Anyone who has dabbled in creative writing has probably heard the expression "show don't tell." This adage encourages us to use images, metaphor, visualization, and the five senses to illustrate what is important in the story as if we were painting a picture with our words. Unfortunately, the facts often do not speak for themselves. While the veracity of your claims is essential, facts only serve as the supporting details for the story, not the hook that makes the story compelling.

Another important aspect of "show don't tell" is to present your story in such a way as to allow the audience to reach their own conclusion rather than "telling" your audience what to believe.

For example, there are over 10,000 different chemicals in cosmetics and personal care products; fewer than 11% of them have ever been tested for effects on human health and the environment.[11] There is mounting evidence that many of these chemicals could be linked to birth defects, miscarriages, and even cancer. The Campaign for Safe Cosmetics[12] is a coalition of women's, environmental justice, and health organizations working to remove known toxins from everyday personal-care products and to create a cancer-free economy.

SmartMeme designed this advertisement for the Safe Cosmetics Coalition.

Re:Imagining Change

The information about cancer-causing cosmetics could be presented with long lists of chemical formulas and graphs of data from toxicity studies, but the Safe Cosmetics Campaign knew that would not communicate the message. A simple values-based narrative and image shows what's at stake and proved much more effective at putting pressure on the cosmetics executives.

The ad *smart*Meme created uses the sympathetic character of a child, and the metaphor of "playing with matches," to invoke the **frame** and values of parental responsibility as a challenge to irresponsible corporate behavior.

The ad appeared in *USA Today* when 20,000 chemical and cosmetics industry leaders were gathered in New York City for a conference. *Smart*Meme chose *USA Today* because the paper is delivered free to every hotel room throughout the conference area. The same day the ad ran, activists from the campaign infiltrated the conference and left copies lying around everywhere. Soon the campaign was the talk of the conference, particularly since the ad named three specific companies and demanded that they reformulate their products to remove toxic chemicals. The ad was targeted to a specific audience of industry leaders, and within several weeks of the conference all three of the companies had started to respond to the campaign's demands.

3.8 Foreshadowing

You throw an anchor into the future you want to build, and you pull yourself along by the chain.
~ John O'Neal

An underlying premise of modern advertising is that people can only go somewhere that they have already been in their minds. This rings true for social change messages too! Our stories must offer a compelling vision of the changes we want.

Foreshadowing is a literary device used by an author to drop subtle hints about plot developments to come later in the story. Incorporating foreshadowing into social change narratives means offering vision, posing a solution to the problem, and constantly referencing the future. How will the conflict come to resolution? What is our vision for a solution to this problem? What does a better world look, feel, and taste like?

BRAND BUSTING

A **brand** is an ongoing and evolving relationship that is shaped by the perceptions of its audience. A brand is not what a company says it is—it's what everyone but the company says it is. So just because a corporation owns a brand, they do not have the power to dictate their **brand**. The **brand** —and its vulnerability to attack in the media— can be an Achilles heel for corporations that rely on their public image to sell products. This is what makes **brand busting**—efforts to associate the **brand** of a specific company with the truth of the injustices they are perpetrating—an effective way to target corporations on social issues.

For example, when the omnipresent McDonald's golden arches were combined with the slogan "McSlavery" by the farmworkers of the Coalition of Immokalee Workers, or Chevron's slogan "People Do" was rewritten to say "Do people kill for oil?" the power of the corporate images were turned against themselves. *Adbusters* magazine founder Kalle Lasn has dubbed this practice of juxtaposing images or co-opting slogans as "culture jamming" or "subvertising"[13]

This smartMeme designed "Mac & Genes box" targeted the Kraft Corporation's flagship brand as part of a national campaign pressuring Kraft to stop using genetically engineered ingredients in their products.

Activists from Chicago's Genewise used Halloween as an opportunity to go Trick-or-Treating in the gated community where Kraft Foods CEO Betsey Holden lived.

In recent years, **brand busting** tactics have been artfully used by corporate accountability campaigns in many sectors. Targeting a brand can be a powerful form of narrative aikido since it uses a corporation's own advertising budget against it by hijacking the imagery already familiar to their customers to present a social change message. Since the long-term effect of attacks on the brand can't be easily measured (and therefore can't be easily dismissed), **brand busting** can help a campaign get the attention of top corporate decision makers.

Average height of a Klamath River dam: **84 feet**

Average height a salmon can jump: **6 feet**

A direct-mail piece made by smartMeme for several Native American tribes and their allies in northern California. It was mailed to all tribal members as part of the campaign to "Bring the Salmon Home" by removing dams on the Klamath River.

When we forecast the future we desire, we invite people to imagine and embrace a visionary solution.

Foreshadowing is essential for taking on one of the most common control mythologies: T.I.N.A., or There-is-No-Alternative. Although this **meme** was coined by Margaret Thatcher—the leader of Britain's Conservative Party throughout the 1980s—it is undoubtedly an ancient strategy of manipulation. The T.I.N.A. narrative acknowledges that the controversial proposal in question is not ideal, but it is the only realistic option, and so it must move forward. This makes it vulnerable to a foreshadowing strategy that offers viable suggestions for other ways of doing things.

With *smart*Meme's support, a coalition of tribes, environmentalists, and commercial fisherman in northern California's Klamath River basin used the **battle of the story** to create a common story that foreshadowed a restored river. The groups had united to demand the removal of outdated dams that had severely impacted both the local indigenous cultures and the commercial fishing industry by limiting salmon habitat. Many of the dams had been in place for over 50 years, and were so accepted as an enduring reality that many residents couldn't imagine that they would ever be removed.

The campaign's **meme** "Bring the Salmon Home" encapsulated the coalition's vision of restoring the salmon's full traditional habitat, and communicated the interdependence between the cultures in the basin (both native and non-native) and a healthy salmon run.

The campaign mail piece is an example of foreshadowing, and effectively **frames** the conflict by showing-not-telling. The mailer doesn't say, "Dams are bad." Rather it explains the impact of the dams on the salmon, and lets the reader draw his or her own conclusions.

The native peoples of the Klamath basin continue to work in alliance with commercial fishermen, environmentalists, and, increasingly, the farming community. Their campaign has shifted the story beyond a debate about whether or not to remove the dams, and into a conversation about how many dams to remove, and how to pay for it.

3.9 Designing a Framing Narrative

Beneath words and logic are emotional connections that largely direct how we use our words and logic.
~ Jane Roberts

Once your group has identified the elements of your story (conflict, characters, images, foreshadowing) the next step is to identify your own underlying assumptions. These assumptions are the shared values (e.g. "equity") and core beliefs (e.g. "All people deserve equal access to opportunity") of your organization, coalition, or alliance.

With your core values clarified and the elements of your story in place, your next step is to synthesize these elements into a framing **narrative**. This overarching narrative should be both compelling to your target audience(s), and challenge the key underlying assumptions that are preventing the dominant **narrative** from changing. This framing **narrative** is an internal, working document that can help your group develop messaging strategy and tactics as you conduct the campaign. The framing **narrative** provides the fodder for talking points, slogans, posters, or other materials.

The process of developing the framing **narrative** (and boiling it down) often requires considerable creativity, experimentation, and collective commitment. The most important thing to remember is that all the elements of the story should reinforce each other to connect seamlessly into a coherent story. As you brainstorm images, develop slogans, and hone your messaging, you must adhere

Re:Imagining Change

to a common **narrative logic**: a coherent, cumulative narrative arc that produces cognitive consonance (as opposed to cognitive dissonance) in the minds of your audience. In other words, the story has got to make sense! The message should be self-evident.

Designing your framing narrative is ultimately a political process: What is inside the frame? Who is not? What must be emphasized and what can't be left out or compromised?

Maintaining a common **narrative logic** takes discipline, especially when you have a diverse group with many creative ideas. You must be vigilant about matching (not mixing) metaphors, choosing the right **meta-verb(s)** (See Section 3.10) to communicate the direction of motion in the story, and developing the appropriate spokespeople as leading characters in the narrative.

Designing your framing narrative is ultimately a political process: What is inside the frame? Who is not? What must be emphasized to offer a new angle on our issue? What can't be left out or compromised as your community wages it's struggle?

This is the hard work of **story-based strategy**. Through this process, your group may choose to cut your issue differently, depending on whom you are trying to influence. These decisions can ripple out through every aspect of the organization. For many grassroots groups with limited resources, this process leads to hard decisions about what to prioritize.

As story-based strategists, we aren't just telling stories—we are changing stories. More often than not, this means challenging stereotypes and dominant cultural assumptions. There are strategic considerations and values-based choices about how to meet short-term campaign objectives, while also achieving longer-term, transformational goals of shifting the dominant culture. These are political calculations you must make within your own circumstance and principles.

This is why *smart*Meme emphasizes that "messaging" is not an afterthought; **story-based strategy** is at the very heart of the work, and the framing **narrative** you develop will have effects on many areas: campaigning, organizing and alliance building, fundraising, morale, group cohesion, etc.

The **battle of the story** tool is not a one-time worksheet–it is a guide for ongoing strategy development as you create your campaign's messages, undertake **interventions**, and encapsulate and spread your story with effective **memes**.

3.10 Action Logic & Meta-Verbs

Change will come. As always, it is just a matter of who determines what that change will be.
~ Winona LaDuke

The concepts of **action logic** and **meta-verbs** are critical to designing your framing narrative. Action logic means that the actions you take have an overarching, self-evident **narrative logic** that speaks for itself and tells a story. The **action logic** is how an action makes sense politically to an outside observer. Having clear **action logic** means that people who witness the action will be able to understand the significance of what is happening, even if they don't have any background information. Good **action logic** can help your message become more memetic and creates the type of powerful stories that move hearts and change minds.

Action logic is frequently summarized through the shorthand of a single action-oriented **meta-verb** that is part of how the action or campaign is publicized. The **meta-verb** you choose —Protest! Rally against! Shut down! Mobilize! Stop! Transform!—will likely become the benchmark of the action's success, not only to the participants, but also to media observers and the general public. Chose your meta-verb(s) wisely! Your **meta-verbs** should communicate a clear **action logic** that anchors your action in a broader **narrative** about your intentions, demands, and world-view.

There are many famous examples of **action logic** with clear **meta-verbs**: The Montgomery Bus Boycott of 1955 ("Boycott!"), The WTO Protests in 1999 ("Shut down the WTO!"), and "Levitate the Pentagon" of 1967. (Well, sometimes the action logic takes some imagination!)

Another example of effective action logic was the "Capitol Climate Action" in March 2009. A coalition of groups fighting global climate change converged on the Capitol Coal Plant in Washington, D.C. The organizers had put out a public call for mass civil disobedience to nonviolently shut down the plant by blocking the gates. This target provided built-in symbolism and implicit story-based strategy: The coal plant provides the Capitol building's electricity and therefore is a potent metaphor for the coal industry's influence on lawmakers on Capitol Hill. The action was designed to draw attention to the fact that our reliance on coal is fueling climate destabilization, and causing massive destruction and human rights abuses: From mountain top removal mining, to water polluting slurry, to poisoning the air for the low income African Americans who live near the plant. Symbolically the plant provided a perfect stage for the action's unfolding **narrative** by offering photogenic images of mass protest shutting down a coal plant, framed between the smokestack and the Capitol dome.

Action logic in practice: National Mobilization for Climate Justice at the Capitol coal-fired power plant in Washington, D.C. (March 2009).

However, while the **action logic** was poetic, the tactic of civil disobedience was distilled to a **meta-verb** of "get arrested," and this logic unraveled when the police declined to arrest anyone. While the action still met its political goals of raising the issue in the national media and building a stronger grassroots movement, for many of the first-time protestors, there was an anti-climactic effect to the lack of arrest.[14] It's important to remember that **framing** isn't just for the media—it's for the base too. Making the frames consistent and resonant—in the narrative and on the ground—is essential for successful, strong, and ongoing mobilization.

3.11 Going Viral: Meme Campaigns

In every ear it spread, on every tongue it grew.
~ Alexander Pope

Once you have used the **battle of the story** tool to deconstruct the story you want to change and design the framing narrative you want to tell, the next step is to figure out how to spread your message. Part of this process is to encapsulate your story in powerful **memes**. Most successful campaigns rely on a few "sticky" **memes** to spread their story and build support amongst a wider audience.

A social change effort focused on spreading a new idea or changing the terms of a debate is essentially a **meme** campaign.[15] Some recent examples of **meme** campaigns include: fair trade, conflict

The Billionaires meme campaign in its 2009 iteration in the healthcare debate.

diamonds, sweatshop-free, living wage, and Live Strong (which popularized the **meme** of colored bracelets).

Thinking of campaigns in terms of **memes** opens up new possibilities and opportunities for organizing. Organizing is about creating a structure to plug people into, and the right **meme** can act as a viral organizing structure. The center of a **meme** campaign is not the headquarters or campaign leadership, and the goal is not building organizational membership in the traditional sense. Instead, the center of the **meme** campaign is the narrative and the contagious self-replicating **meme** capsules that spread the story.

The **meme**, by its very nature, mutates over time and expresses itself in myriad formations as it moves through existing networks and creates new ones. A good **meme** campaign is designed so that people can take the **meme** and "run with it" at the grassroots level without the **meme** (and message) losing its intent and integrity.

At its core, an effective **meme** campaign requires strong grassroots organizing and a flexible, network-based structure in order to flourish. The primary role of the network's main nodes (which are likely organizers, but may be unexpected people, media sources, or events) is to encourage the replication of the **meme**. Organizers act as weavers of the decentralized network web, spreading information, connecting people, gathering feedback, and offering support.

A great example of a **meme** campaign was created in the lead-up to the 2000 elections, when economic justice activists set out to show the need for campaign finance reform by exposing the undue influence of big money contributors on both parties. They created *Billionaires for Bush (or Gore)*, a faux movement of billionaires. They took on billionaire personas like Phil T. Rich and Hallie Burton who would protest at protests and get major media attention with messages like "Widen the income gap" and "Tax the poor, not us!"

Billionaires for Bush (or Gore) was essentially a street theater concept to transmit a **meme** suggesting that Big Money owned

Re:Imagining Change

both candidates. The organizers provided some basic resources—core messages, costuming tips, and adaptable guerilla theater scenarios that would allow the **meme** to spread virally without losing its core meaning. The oxymoron of billionaires protesting, as well as the "Bush OR Gore" tagline, was so at odds with the conventional **framing** of the election that it captured the attention of people and the media. The campaign itself was particularly effective because it was accessible: anyone could become a Billionaire. Activists around the country tailored the tactic to their own needs throughout the election, and spread the **meme** with in-character radio spots, protests, and stunts at candidate events—delivering a hard-hitting political message with humor.[17]

In 2004 they were back as *Billionaires for Bush*, with slogans like "Four More Wars" and "Leave No Billionaire Behind." The campaign mobilized thousands of people and attracted massive media attention using humor and storytelling. The Billionaires **meme** continues to be a useful platform for creative organizing and has morphed into other campaigns like *Billionaires for Big Oil*, *Billionaires for Bailouts*, and *Billionaires for Wealthcare (Not Healthcare)*.

Critical Mass bike rides are a meme campaign that has spread around the globe over the past decade. The simple idea of the meme is to create a ritual where bike riders gather at a specific time and place (often the last Friday of the month) to cycle en masse through rush-hour traffic. It was originally intended to build visibility for the bike community and demand changes in transit policy to make cities less car-dependent and more bike-friendly. Military analysts speculating on the potential battlefield applications of decentralized decision-making have cited Critical Mass.[16] This shows that leaderless movements built around a meme that is flexible and adaptive to local conditions can attract attention from some powerful quarters.

Those who profess to favor freedom and yet depreciate agitation, are people who want crops without ploughing the ground; they want rain without thunder and lightning; they want the ocean without the roar of its many waters. The struggle may be a moral one, or it may be a physical one, or it may be both. But it must be a struggle. Power concedes nothing without a demand; it never has and it never will.

~ Frederick Douglass

4. Points of Intervention

4.1 Social Change as Intervention

Imagination is intervention, an act of defiance. It alters belief.
~ David Mura

So you want to take action to change a story that is hurting your community...but how? Whether you're targeting a specific brand narrative put forward by a powerful corporation or resisting racist policies rooted in generations of oppressive assumptions, it can be a daunting task to take your story off the flipchart and into the streets.

You have used the **battle of the story** tool to deconstruct the story you want to change and to synthesize your framing narrative into some potent memes you want to spread. The next dimension of the **story-based strategy** model is taking action at **points of intervention (POI)**.

*Smart*Meme defines **intervention** as: an action meant to change the course of events. Intervention is deliberate interference or interaction with a previously existing narrative, audience, social structure, system, venue, or space.

Points of intervention are specific places in a system where an action can effectively interrupt and influence the narrative of that system and build momentum for change.

Social movements traditionally

When a direct action intervention is effective, it shifts power relationships in the moment it is happening and also builds lasting movement by leaving an imprint in our imaginations of new possibilities.

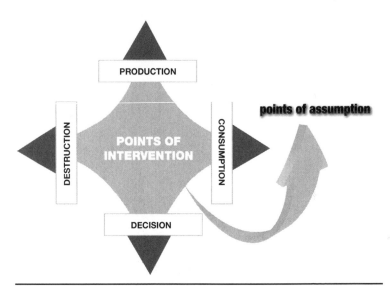

Points of Intervention are the places in a system where taking action can make change. Social movements have a long history of taking action where production, consumption, destruction, or decision-making is happening. **Story-based strategy** helps us expand these efforts to envision interventions into the narratives that shape popular understanding by taking action at the **point of assumption**.

intervene at physical points in the systems that shape our lives, otherwise known as "direct action." The locations of these types of interventions have included: the **point of production** where goods are produced (such as a factory or laboratory), the **point of destruction** where resources are extracted or pollution is dumped (such as a logging road or toxic waste site), the **point of consumption** where products are purchased (such as a chain store or a lunch counter) and the point of **decision** where the **power-holders** are located (such as a corporate headquarters or a congressional office).

Direct action is an age-old method of taking action to make positive changes in the world, from a community putting up their own radio transmitter to give voice to local residents, to mass civil disobedience to shut down a corporate war profiteer. Direct action is a general term for any action where people step out of their traditional, scripted roles (be it as passive consumers, marginalized nobodies, or apathetic spectators) and challenge the dominant

Re:Imagining Change

expectation of obedience. When a direct action intervention is effective, it shifts power relationships in the moment it is happening and also builds lasting movement by leaving an imprint in our imaginations of new possibilities. Direct action is often a tactic within a broader strategy, but it also represents a political ethic of creating fundamental change at the deepest levels of power relations.

> *Narrative Power Analysis reminds us that interventions at physical points can go beyond disrupting a system to pose a deeper challenge to its underlying assumptions and legitimacy.*

Social change forces don't have equal access to the privately owned infrastructure of mass media and communication, so we need to tell our story creatively through our actions. **Narrative power analysis** reminds us that interventions at physical points can go beyond disrupting a system to pose a deeper challenge to its underlying assumptions and legitimacy. This holds true for a physical system such as sweatshop manufacturing or an ideological system like racism, sexism, or homophobia.

Through the lens of **story-based strategy,** we can see **points of intervention** that operate not only in physical space, but also in **narrative space. Story-based strategy** is based in the notion that narratives operate on underlying assumptions, and so in order to change stories, we need to shift assumptions. Actions at a **point of assumption** are actions with the explicit goal of **changing the story.** These types of actions can often be combined with an action at a physical point to make the intervention more effective.

The 1937 Flint sit-down strike is one of the great moments in U.S. labor history. By occupying and stopping production at three General Motors factories for over six weeks, workers won recognition of their union, the United Auto Workers.

4.2 Point of Production

If the workers took a notion they could stop all speeding trains;
Every ship upon the ocean they can tie with mighty chains.
Every wheel in the creation, every mine and every mill;
Fleets and armies of the nation, will at their command stand still.
~ Joe Hill, labor organizer executed by the state of Utah in 1915

Action at the **point of production** is the foundational insight of the labor movement. Workers organize to target the economic system where it directly affects them, and where that system is most vulnerable—at the site of production. Strikes, picket lines, work slowdowns, and factory take-overs are all point of production actions. Other **points of production** are factory farms or facilities where new products or technologies are created.

Members of the Penan indigenous community in the Malaysian state of Sarawak blockade an illegal logging road built in their traditional homelands. The Penan's movement to protect the rainforests helped inspire North American direct action techniques of tree sitting and road blockades to stop industrial logging.

4.3 Point of Destruction

So bleak is the picture... that the bulldozer and not the atomic bomb may turn out to be the most destructive invention of the 20th century.
~ Philip Shabecoff

The **point of destruction** is where harm or an injustice is actually occurring in its most blatant form. Intervention at this point can halt the practice in the moment, as well as dramatize the larger **battle of the story** around the issue. It could be the place where the raw materials to fuel manufacturing come from, such as mining, fossil-fuel drilling, or logging. The **point of destruction** can also be the place where the waste from the **point of production** is dumped—an effluent pipe in a river, diesel emissions along a trucking route, or a leaky toxic waste dump. From remote rural and wilderness areas, to polluted inner cities, impacted communities frequently mobilize to take action at the **point of destruction.**

Re:Imagining Change

It is critical to bring public attention to the **point of destruction** because it is almost always (by design) out of the public eye. In many cases, the **point of destruction** is made invisible by distance, oppressive assumptions, or ignorance. Impacted communities generally have less political power, so **point of destruction** actions are most effective when they capture public attention or are supported with solidarity actions at other **points of intervention.**

4.4 Point of Consumption

Consumerism turns us all into junk-ies.
~ Earon Davis

The **point of consumption** is the location of everyday interaction with a product or service. It becomes particularly relevant when the product in question is linked to injustice. **Point of consumption** actions are the traditional arena of consumer boycotts and storefront demonstrations. Examples include: sit-ins at the Woolworth's lunch counters to protest legalized racial segregation, efforts to spread **memes** like "sweat-shop free," "dolphin-safe tuna," and "fair trade" in the marketplace, or protesting oil wars at gas stations. The **point of consumption** is often the most visible **point of intervention** in our consumerist society. **Point of consumption** actions can also be a good way to get the attention of corporate **power-holders** when lawmakers aren't listening.

Over the past two decades, "market campaigns" have emerged as a model that aims to shift the dynamics of an industry by shutting down the market for destructive products.[1] This strategy goes beyond **brand busting** and operates with a comprehensive analysis of the

Human rights and economic justice activists protest sweatshops at Gap stores. The globalized economy relocates the vast majority of manufacturing to the Global South—meaning poor wages and abusive working conditions are far from the public eye in the U.S. Actions at the point of consumption can illuminate injustices at other points in the system.

marketplace and its key institutional players. Campaigners have effectively pressured retailers, investors, shareholders, wholesale suppliers, subcontractors, and other links in the chain of production, destruction, and consumption, to meet their demands. Human rights activists have confronted retailers selling sweatshop products. Forest defenders have pressured companies to stop purchasing wood and paper from old growth forests. Public health crusaders have targeted cosmetics and chemical companies with actions aimed at impacting brand profiles and eroding market share. Intervention at the **point of consumption** is often a key element of a market campaign.

4.5 Point of Decision

> Change means movement. Movement means friction. Only in the frictionless vacuum of a nonexistent abstract world can movement or change occur without that abrasive friction of conflict.
> ~ Saul Alinsky

The **point of decision** is the location of the **power-holders** who can meet the campaign's demand. Whether taking over a slumlord's office, bursting into a corporate boardroom, or protesting at the state capital, many successful campaigns have used some form of action at the **point of decision** to put pressure on the key decision makers.

Sometimes a **point of decision** action can **reframe** an issue by unmasking hidden interests and challenging assumptions about who is to blame for a problem. Some successful examples include: protesting global poverty at World Bank meetings, calling for an end to agricultural sweatshops at the fast food chain Burger King headquarters, and targeting executives at an

*Over 50,000 people protested at the Seattle meetings of the World Trade Organization in November 1999 because they understood that the unelected and unaccountable WTO was going to be making decisions that affected their lives. These protests illuminated a new **point of decision** in the global economy.*

auto show for their failure to address global warming emissions. In these cases, **intervention** at the **point of decision** also aims at the **point of assumption**.

4.6 Point of Assumption

People do not change with the times, they change the times.
~ PK Shaw

The traditional four **points of intervention** are interventions in physical space. These points focus on the tangible gears of the machinery that drives injustice, oppression, and destruction. Historically, social movements have succeeded in winning changes when these physical actions have also changed the story around the issue. This means **reframing** the problem, building a base of committed people, and winning a critical mass of support for solutions. The end result is a re-patterning of popular consciousness to embrace a new story.

> Shifting the debate, moving the center of gravity, and changing the story are all metaphors to describe a cultural shift that creates the space for political changes to emerge.

Shifting the debate, moving the center of gravity, and **changing the story** are all metaphors that describe a cultural shift that creates the space for political changes to emerge. **Story-based strategy** is an exploration of how social movements can operate in the realm of narrative to create a shared story for interpreting political issues that inform the understanding of a critical mass of society.[2]

Applying a **narrative power analysis** helps us scout for the specific **points of intervention** in the narratives that we want to change; this is fundamentally about identifying and targeting underlying assumptions that sustain the status quo. These interventions aim to pass through the filters of their

INTERVENTION AT POINTS OF ASSUMPTION
▶ Offer new futures
▶ Reframe debates
▶ Subvert spectacles
▶ Repurpose existing narratives
▶ Make the invisible visible

audience and change their story. We call this action at the **point of assumption.**

Assumptions are the unstated parts of the story that you have to believe in order to believe the story is true. They are the glue that holds the narrative together, and when they are exposed and found in contradiction to the lived experience or values of the audience, they are vulnerable. Action to expose and target these assumptions can **change the story. Point of assumption** actions can take many forms: exposing hypocrisy or lies, **reframing** the issue, amplifying the voices of previously silenced characters in the story, or offering an alternative vision.

4.7 Offering New Futures

> A pile of rocks ceases to be a pile of rocks when somebody contemplates it with the idea of a cathedral in mind.
> ~ Antoine de St. Exupéry

One place to find **points of assumption** is at the point in the story where the endings become contestable—where effective action can forecast a different future. Such vision-driven actions are not new, and arguably have always been a staple of successful social change. However, by understanding them as interventions at a **point of assumption** we can focus on what has made them successful and work to replicate those aspects.

One of the most common assumptions in **power-holders'** stories is some version of the "There Is No Alternative" (TINA)[3] **control myth** (See Section 3.8). In these instances, the effective articulation of a plausible story about a different future can be a powerful challenge to the status quo narrative. Actions that contest a seemingly pre-determined future are one type of action at the **point of assumption.**

A few examples of this type of intervention include:

♦ Activists confront biotechnology and the corporate takeover of the food system by transforming an empty lot into a garden where neighbors can grow healthy, organic food.

♦ Homes Not Jails activists challenge city officials to provide more housing for low income families by occupying an abandoned building to create a place for people to live.

♦ Public housing residents pushing for a better childcare space take action at the local government office, and instead of just doing a sit-in, they transform the office into the day-care center the community needs.

The fundamental question for these types of actions is: "What if...?" Even if the action is a symbolic foreshadowing (rather than a concrete plan), it can still challenge the status quo narrative by offering glimpses of alternatives. This type of intervention can open up the political imagination to the possibility of a real solution. Intervention at the **point of assumption** can reclaim public space for the discussion of a problem untethered from the confines of the **power-holder's framing**—introducing new ideas, new possibilities, new solutions, even new identities and ways of being.

4.8 Reframing Debates

Change looks impossible when you start, and looks inevitable after you've finished.
~ Bob Hunter

In 1981, environmentalists in the western United States were fighting to defend wilderness areas from the intrusions of industrial mega-projects like giant dams. The newly formed radical ecology network Earth First! was thinking bigger than the usual protest at the **point of destruction.** They wanted to challenge the deep-seated narrative of technological progress "conquering" nature. They knew that they had to confront the assumption that industrial mega-projects like giant dams were permanent immovable structures, and foreshadow a future of undoing damage to the planet. They chose intervention at the

In 1981, environmental visionaries "cracked" the Glen Canyon Dam to challenge the assumption that mega-development projects had to be permanent. This intervention helped **reframe** the debate around wilderness preservation.

Glen Canyon Dam, the second highest concrete arch dam in the United States that dams the Colorado River in Arizona.

On the anniversary of the Glen Canyon Dam's opening, they unfurled a huge black plastic banner down the face of the dam, visually creating a giant crack, and foreshadowing a day when dams would be removed and rivers restored.[4]

Until their iconic action, the industrial paradigm of dominating nature had rendered the question of removing a mega-dam unthinkable in the public debate. The "cracking" action challenged that assumption and created a new political space. Twenty-five years later, struggles against dams continue, but today, dam removal is increasingly embraced as a solution to restore damaged fishing stocks and watersheds.

4.9 Subverting Spectacles

*Iraq Veterans were among the over 5,000 people who participated in the **Turn Your Back on Bush** mobilization at the 2005 inauguration.*

Disneyland is presented as imaginary in order to make us believe that the rest is real.
~ Jean Baudrillard

In the wake of the 2004 U.S. election, some creative organizers saw the opportunity to mobilize the disillusioned into the longer-term progressive movement. *Turn Your Back on Bush* was born: a **point of assumption** action organized by Action Mill (www.actionmill.com), with support from *smart*Meme.[5]

It was clear that the Bush administration's draconian security measures would limit protest along the 2005 Bush Inaugural parade route, and that it would be difficult for traditional protest tactics to break out of the media's existing **frame**.

So their action mobilized over 5,000 people to covertly enter the security zone, line the parade route, and then turn their backs on the Presidential motorcade as it passed. This form of symbolic protest may seem trivial (given the scale of Bush's crimes against humanity), but it was an action that was targeting a specific **point of assumption**: the Bush narrative that the election had provided a "mandate."

Re:Imagining Change

SELLING THE WORLD BANK ON EBAY

In 2004 activists at the World Bank Bonds Boycott teamed up with *smartMeme* to expose the World Bank's role in perpetuating poverty and injustice. Protest outside the Bank's annual meetings had peaked several years earlier so it was time for a new way to hijack the spectacle of media attention around the Bank's annual fall meeting. So *smartMeme* posted the World Bank for sale on the online auction website eBay. The action logic of "Selling The World Bank on eBay" was a humorous way to point out that, contrary to its stated mission of ending poverty, the Bank is actually for sale to the highest bidder. The posting on eBay described the World Bank as "Antiquated: does not work" and generated headlines like: "World Bank for sale on eBay - Activists say the bank 'will do a lot less harm to the world gathering dust in your attic" (CNN) and 'World Bank' Bidding Starts at 30 Cents on eBay (Reuters). The media stunt used carefully crafted language on the eBay post to embed the substance of the issues into the action. For instance, the asking price was $0.30, the average hourly wage of a sweatshop worker in Haiti. This action used a humorous and very clear action logic to engage a serious topic and garner high profile global press coverage for the campaign.

The **action logic** of turning your back was clear. It was carried out by thousands of people representing constituencies that Bush was claiming to speak for: veterans, military families, farmers, fire fighters, and people of faith. The action communicated a mass symbolic withdrawal of consent for Bush's presidency.

The action effectively subverted the spectacle of Bush's grand triumph and launched a counter story about the broad base of resistance to his policies. The action received major media coverage around the world, and even entered **popular culture** consciousness as the subject of a skit on the popular television program *Saturday Night Live*.

The action mobilized over 5,000 people to covertly enter the security zone, line the parade route and then turn their backs on the presidential motorcade as it passed.

U.S. athletes Tommie Smith and Juan Carlos captured global attention by making a Black Power raised-fist salute on the medal stand at the 1968 Olympics in Mexico City. This famous action subverted the spectacle of the medal ceremony to make a statement rejecting racism and oppression. Both of them were stripped of their medals, although years later they were reinstated. Spectacles are everywhere in the popular culture, and can provide opportunities for point of assumption interventions.

Turn Your Back on Bush's simple and unique **action logic** allowed the protest to go viral as a **meme**, and reports of people greeting Bush with the turned backs of protest emerged from around the country and the world.

4.10 Repurposing Pop(ular) Culture Narratives

If there's any hope for a revolution in America, it lies in getting Elvis Presley to become Che Guevara.
~ Phil Ochs

In a critique of the media-saturation of U.S. culture, it is easy to forget that **pop culture** means popular. It is marketed en masse, creating familiarity with the characters, images and plots of contemporary **pop culture** products such as movies, television programs, commercials, internet sites, popular music, and viral videos. **Popular culture** can provide unique opportunities for social change messages to "hitch a ride" on specific **memes**, metaphors, and cultural narratives.

> Popular culture can provide unique opportunities for social change messages to "hitch a ride" on specific memes, metaphors, and cultural narratives.

Popular culture narratives are like rivers running through mainstream culture. If a campaign can craft a message that floats on the river—without the message being

Re:Imagining Change

trivialized or submerged—then the campaign can repurpose that existing narrative.

The imagery, characters, and narratives of popular Hollywood movies like *The Matrix, The Lord of the Rings,* and *Harry Potter* have all been borrowed and repurposed for social change ends.

Activists used this strategy in a banner-hang action to protest the U.S. invasion of Iraq in 2003. "Frodo has failed—Bush has the ring!" was the slogan seen by thousands on their morning commutes on Interstate 40 in Knoxville, Tennessee.

The banner message played on the pre-release marketing hype of the second installment in the blockbuster *Lord of the Rings* trilogy. The pun was funny, and so the action was a topic on morning radio call-in shows and news programs.

The action caused such a stir that the company whose ad appeared on the billboard—the restaurant chain Hooters—attempted to cash in on the publicity by allowing the banner to stay up. They played on the story by placing ads on their local restaurant kiosks saying, "Frodo has Failed. Hooters has the WING!" in order to advertise their chicken wings.

This was ironic (since part of the reason the activists chose that particular billboard

In 2003 activists from Katuah Earth First! in Knoxville, TN won popular support and massive media coverage for their anti-war action by tapping into the popular narrative of the Lord of the Rings *movies.*

was to protest Hooters' infamous sexism), but it spurred another round of media conversation and water cooler jokes about the action. The activists (one of whom was a *smart*Meme training alumna!) were not arrested, and the banner stayed up for a number of days and was seen by thousands of commuters.

To someone unfamiliar with J.R.R. Tolkien's books or the Hollywood movies based on them, the banner message is meaningless. But if you know the code you can easily decipher that the banner means, "Bush is the ultimate evil and is a threat to the entire world." (Imagine the response if the activists had chosen to write that message!) This example demonstrates how **pop culture** can offer us detailed cultural codes that can help popularize messages that otherwise would not get by the filters of a mass audience (See Section 2.5 for more on **narrative filters**).

The danger in appropriating **popular culture** narratives is that the references are ever changing and ephemeral. Some iconic images and narratives become cultural touchstones that can stand the test of time, while others are fleeting and are quickly replaced by a flurry of media promoting the next Hollywood blockbuster or consumer product. **Pop culture** may create a common **meme** for millions of people, but it will soon be yesterday's joke if you don't move fast. In this age of niche marketing and **narrowcasting,** it's important to understand who knows the specific **pop culture** code you're using and who doesn't.

4.11 Making the Invisible visible

When you change the way you look at things, the things you look at change.
~ Max Planck

After a **story-based strategy** session in 2007, Iraq Veterans Against the War (IVAW) decided to take direct action at the **point of assumption** and experiment with an intervention in American iconography. Their goal was to **change the story** from "we are at WAR in Iraq," and therefore must stay until we "win," to "this is an OCCUPATION of Iraq," and the presence of U.S. troops is making the situation worse. They wanted the U.S. public to understand that occupations inevitably create violence and can never be "won." The group decided to show not tell what occupation really is. They called their series of actions *Operation First Casualty*, after the notion that the first casualty of war is truth.

IVAW intervened with reality street theater: veterans in uniform went on patrol in U.S. cities as if they were in Iraq, including simulating crowd control actions and civilian arrest operations. The actions were an effort to show the U.S. public

Iraq Veterans Against the War make the invisible impacts of the U.S. occupation visible to passersby, using the iconic backdrops of Washington and New York. Operation First Casualty was their intervention to re-pattern assumptions about what the U.S. occupation of Iraq really looks like.

what occupation looks like and feels like, and to create cognitive dissonance by using the setting of iconic places like Times Square in New York City and the National Mall in Washington, D.C.

IVAW knew that simply telling people that the occupation is undemocratic and oppressive wasn't enough. They wanted to give the public an experience of occupation by creating memorable images of what it would look like in the U.S. These interventions powerfully demonstrated the principle of making the invisible visible. While the action took an emotional toll for some of the vets who participated, it was a radical act of real world **culture jamming.** *Operation First Casualty* dramatically contrasted IVAW's first-hand experiences of Iraq with the Bush administration's propaganda.

THE POINTS OF INTERVENTION	IDENTIFY THE POINT	INTERVENTION IDEAS
POINT OF PRODUCTION The realm of strikes, picket lines. Factory occupations, crop lands, and agricultural actions, etc.		
POINT OF DESTRUCTION Resource extraction such as logging, mines, etc. Point of toxic discharge, etc.		
POINT OF CONSUMPTION The realm of consumer boy-cotts and markets campaigns. Places were customers can be reached. Chain stores, super-markets, etc.		
POINT OF DECISION Location of targeted decision maker. Corporate H.Q., slumlord's office, etc.		
POINT OF ASSUMPTION Challenging underlying as-sumptions & control mytholo-gies, subverting spectacles, contesting futures, intervening in popular culture…		

2. Narrative Power Analysis

Our strategy should be not only to confront empire, but to lay siege to it. To deprive it of oxygen. To shame it. To mock it. With our art, our music, our literature, our stubbornness, our joy, our brilliance, our sheer relentlessness—and our ability to tell our own stories. Stories that are different from the ones we're being brainwashed to believe.

~ Arundhati Roy at the 2003 World Social Forum

5. Changing the Story

Opportunities multiply as they are seized.
~ Sun Tzu

5.1 Strategic Improvisation

Thus far, this manual has explored and enunciated various aspects of a **story-based strategy** approach. The foundational framework is a **narrative power analysis**: viewing social change efforts and power relationships through the lens of story. The **elements of story** are a tool to deconstruct the narratives we want to change, and construct the story of our own vision. We have also examined **memes,** and looked at how they can carry **control mythologies** as well as encapsulate and spread social change messages.

In Section III, we distinguished between mobilizing and persuasion narratives and offered techniques for waging the **battle of the story.** Section IV examined the **points of intervention** and presented ideas for action at the **point of assumption** to **reframe** narratives and shift popular understanding of an issue.

This manual is only an introduction to these ideas, and there is certainly a need for deeper thinking and many more applications and experiments to try out in the field. The methodologies in this manual are most effective when used together,

> Strategy is not a rigid set of instructions. Effective strategic practice requires reflective, thoughtful leadership, and making choices when faced with developing situations. In other words, there is always an improvisational element.

but different campaigns and situations will require different applications.

We believe that social change innovation is emergent and thus requires the practice of improvisation. Effective **change agents** bring a background of skills and experience, a strategic framework, and an awareness of the present conditions to inform how they act within a range of options that best fit the situation. To be successful at improvisation (be it in cooking, hip-hop, or activism) requires resourcefulness, creativity, and a stash of good ideas. Improvisational forays are often the edges of yet unseen innovations.

*Smart*Meme's approach recognizes that a successful strategy is not only a premeditated plan that emerges from analysis—it also must evolve in a real-world context of changing conditions. Strategy is not a rigid set of instructions. Effective strategic practice requires reflective, thoughtful leadership, and making choices when faced with developing situations. In other words, there is always an improvisational element.

In this spirit, we want to point out that there is no one sure-fire prescription to design and implement a **story-based strategy**. There is no one magic **meme** or universal blueprint for success. The term **story-based strategy** may be new, but the techniques of storytelling are ancient, and the body of work on social movement strategy is vast.

In this section, we present four case studies that exemplify some of the methods of **story-based strategy** we've been discussing. First, a widely known historic example: the Greenpeace "Save the Whales" campaign. Two other case studies come from the *smart*Meme collective's own work applying **story-based strategy** on the ground with the grassroots organizing campaigns of Rural Vermont and Protect Our Waters. Both offer rich examples of the **battle of the story** in action. The final case study is a campaign that *smart*Meme has not been intimately involved in shaping, but we have been honored to support. We have learned a great deal from the Coalition of Immokalee Workers and their successful efforts to win better wages and working conditions for farmworkers in southwest Florida. Each of these examples offers lessons and inspiration about how to apply **story-based strategy** ideas in real world struggles. We hope these stories inspire you to experiment with narrative in your own efforts to change the world.

5.2 CASE STUDY
Greenpeace: Save the Whales

Greenpeace's "Save the Whales" campaign is a great example of **changing the story,** and is credited with shifting public perceptions of whales.[1] When Greenpeace began the campaign in the mid-1970s, industrial whaling was driving many species of whale to the point of extinction, and there was little public awareness about the issue. Greenpeace was a new organization, and they had already successfully mixed media-savvy, nonviolent direct action, and the Quaker tradition of "bearing witness" into a grassroots campaign against nuclear testing. When they set out to challenge the whaling industry, they knew they would need to push their new tactics even further. Greenpeace knew they could never intervene at every **point of destruction** and save every whale, so they set out to change the way the **dominant culture** thought of whaling—to **change the story** of whaling.

> Greenpeace knew they could never intervene at every point of destruction and save every whale. So they set out to change the way the dominant culture thought of whaling—to change the story of whaling.

Greenpeace campaigners asked themselves, what is the popular understanding of whaling, and where did it come from? They realized that people knew relatively little about whales, and that much of what they thought they knew came from a book that was commonly read in high schools: Herman Melville's 19th-century novel *Moby Dick*. The vision of whaling presented in *Moby Dick* depicts heroic whalers taking to the sea in tiny boats and risking their lives to battle giant, evil whales.

But by the late 20th century, whaling was an industrial enterprise. Giant factory whaling ships dwarfed the endangered mammals, slaughtering

> Greenpeace's "Save the Whales" campaign is a great example of changing the story, and is credited with shifting public perceptions of whales.

Images such as these reflected popular perceptions of whales and whaling before the campaign.

In this new narrative, whales were not big and evil; rather it was the giant whaling ships that were the dangerous monsters.

them en masse in a manner that was neither heroic nor risky. Greenpeace knew they had to expose the invisible reality of industrial whaling. Greenpeace set out to create a series of "image events"—**spectacles** that told a dramatic story—which could replace the **popular culture's** concept of whaling.

The iconic images they created were of Greenpeace activists in small Zodiac boats placing themselves directly between the giant factory whaling ships and the whales. It was dangerous and activists did get hurt. Greenpeace used the first generation of handheld video cameras to record their attempts to get between the harpoons and the whales, and succeeded in getting the images broadcast around the world.[2]

This intervention at the **point of destruction** created an effective direct action at the **point of assumption**. The actions

Greenpeace activists confront a factory whaling ship.

Re:Imagining Change

showed it was the activists, not the whalers, who were the courageous people on small boats risking their lives—not to kill whales, but to save them. In this new narrative, whales were not big and evil; rather it was the giant whaling ships that were the dangerous monsters. The whales were the helpless victims and became sympathetic and worthy of protection. The Greenpeace activists (and the burgeoning environmental movement they represented) became the heroes. The story changed and the roles of hero, victim, and villain shifted.

Greenpeace activists in Zodiac boats place themselves between the whaling ships and the whales.

The campaign won the **battle of the story** of whaling, and ultimately succeeded in securing international treaties to protect endangered whales. Unfortunately, in recent years, whaling interests have exploited loopholes in these treaties. Activists are once again campaigning to protect whales. However, because of this successful **story-based strategy,** these new campaigns have the power of public support on their side.

Greenpeace activists are shot with water cannons as they fight to save a captured whale. Images such as these helped replace the Moby Dick mythology and shift the hero/victim/villain triangle of the story.

The Farmer Protection Act

Keeps Corporate Lawyers from Having a Field Day

Genetically engineered seed contracts force farmers
to accept all liability for any contamination problems.

The Farmer Protection Act shifts this liability back
to the biotechnology corporations - where it belongs.

If there is no problem, then the bill burdens no one.

If there is a problem, it protects all Vermont farmers.

**Vermont's Top Concern Should Be Family Farmers,
not Biotech's Bottom Line.**

For more information www.ruralvermont.org 802-223-7222
Ad designed by smartMeme - www.smartmeme.com

Elmer the scarecrow driving corporate lawyers off the family farm. The face of the middle lawyer has an uncanny similarity to Monsanto's chief lobbyist in the state. (Just a coincidence, of course...)

5.3 CASE STUDY
Rural Vermont: One Contaminated Farm Is One Too Many

Starting in 2004, *smart*Meme partnered with the grassroots economic justice organization Rural Vermont, a membership organization led by family farmers. Rural Vermont was campaigning against genetically engineered (GE) agriculture. This rapidly spreading and untested technology poses threats to family farmers, human health, and the environment.[3] *Smart*Meme supported Rural Vermont as a key constituent-led, membership organization that was tackling this global issue at the local level.

In 2004, Rural Vermont won successful passage of the Farmers' Right to Know GE Seed Labeling and Registration Act. This law puts the USDA organic standards' definition of "genetically modified" into Vermont statute, and requires that GE seeds be clearly labeled as such. This was a tremendous victory. With GE defined on the books, they had the ability to move the issue further.

There was a serious danger that pollen from genetically engineered (GE) crops planted on one farm could drift and contaminate neighboring farms that had not chosen to plant GE crops. The giant biotech companies like Monsanto, who own the patents to the GE seeds, were covering up the contamination issue. Their tactic was to sue farmers whose crops had been contaminated for "patent infringement" and "unauthorized pirating" of their copyrighted technology.

Re:Imagining Change

The farmers of Vermont decided to stand up to this corporate bullying and demand that the state legislature pass a law to hold the manufacturers of genetically engineered seeds accountable for "drift" and contamination. This would mean that if a farmer's field was contaminated, instead of suing his neighbor he could hold the real culprit accountable—the patent-holding corporations like Monsanto.

When GE crop contamination was uncovered on an organic farm in the state the campaign rallied around the slogan: "One contaminated farm is one too many." Rural Vermont organized farmers and local-food advocates to pressure state lawmakers to adopt policies to protect farmers' interests. They called their proposed legislation the Farmer Protection Act, a **framing** that stuck throughout the campaign and connected corporate liability with protecting farmers.

Rural Vermont's **story-based strategy** used many tactics: letter writing, rallies, media, print advertisements, and nonviolent direct actions. The campaign narrative kept the focus on the farmers—the impacted sympathetic characters—and was based in Vermont's rural culture of family farming. An

As the meme spread, farmers and their allies gathered across the state to display support for the Farmer Protection Act by making scarecrows.

The Farmer Protection Act

Good for All Vermont Farmers No Matter Which Way the Wind Blows

The Farmer Protection Act

Leaves Corporate Lawyers with No Place to Hide

Vermont's Top Concern Should Be Family Farmers, not Biotech's Bottom Line.

Inexpensive ads ran in local papers to coincide with appearances by Elmer and his growing scarecrow army at the statehouse.

FARMER PROTEST

AP Photo/Toby Talbot

Protesters stand in front of the Statehouse in Montpelier Tuesday during a march to support the Farmer Protection Act and to protest what they call the Agency of Agriculture's pro-industry stance on GMO seeds.

Elmer, the scarecrow featured in the ads, began to show up in real life at the statehouse.

The campaign narrative kept the focus on the farmers—the impacted sympathetic characters—and was based on Vermont's rural culture of family farming.

aggressive media strategy and emphasis on popular education made "genetic engineering" a household term across the state.

Together, Rural Vermont and *smart*Meme developed a meme campaign that anchored the narrative by promoting the scarecrow as an icon of the campaign. The scarecrow was a powerful symbol because it embodied the idea of protecting the farmers and the crops from predators. It told the story that Rural Vermont was protecting the seeds against the latest threat from Monsanto.

The **meme** was launched with a series of inexpensive advertisements featuring "Elmer" the scarecrow. Elmer was depicted confronting corporate lawyers, and these images framed the conflict as local farmers vs. out-of-state corporate interests.

The farmers were explicit that they did not want to be cast as the victims, and so the campaign images depicted the scarecrow as powerful. The images show the scarecrow chasing corporate lawyers out of the pasture, using a light-saber-like flashlight to catch them in the hen house, and standing proud against the backdrop of an iconic Vermont landscape. In this way, the **story-based strategy** was **reframing** who had the power in the story, and foreshadowing victory.

As the campaign gained ground, Elmer the scarecrow mascot showed up in real life at the statehouse, along roads across the countryside, and at Rural Vermont rallies. The **meme** spread, carrying Rural Vermont's story of protecting local agriculture and the rural way of life. Farmers and their allies gathered across the state to make and display scarecrows as a show of public support for the campaign.

All of Rural Vermont's hard work and organizing paid off and the Vermont state legislature passed the *Farmer Protection Act* in 2005. It was a major victory for the coalition of concerned Vermonters who rallied behind the scarecrow. Unfortunately, despite thousands of calls to the Republican governor's office in support of the bill, he vetoed it in 2006.

This campaign provides the movement against genetically engineered agriculture an inspiring model, linking innovative policy work with grassroots organizing. Rural Vermont continues their work for "living soils, thriving farms, and healthy communities."

5.4 CASE STUDY
Protect Our Waters: Our Most Precious Resource

Around the world, transnational companies are moving to aggressively privatize water and turn what has historically been a shared life-sustaining common resource into a lucrative commodity. Bottled water is big business, with global sales revenues approaching $100 billion dollars and continuing to grow.[4] Ironically, most of this market is in affluent countries like the U.S. that generally have safe tap water available for free.

In 2007, community residents of the Mt. Shasta area of Northern California invited *smart*Meme to support their efforts to prevent the construction of the nation's largest water bottling plant. Nestlé Corporation—the world's largest water company, based in Switzerland—was going to build the plant in the small town of McCloud. The company had been preparing the plans for several years and had convinced the five-person local Community Services District to sign a 100-year contract before there was any public debate. In response, local residents formed the Protect Our Waters Coalition (POW) to protect the ecological, cultural, and economic integrity of Mt. Shasta's unique headwater areas for future generations. The coalition brought together the McCloud Watershed Council and two locally active sporting and conservation organizations—California Trout and Trout Unlimited.

*Smart*Meme worked with the residents and their allies to provide training, facilitate group strategy sessions, and apply a nar-

Siskiyou County residents mobilize to protect their water and way of life.

This image created by smartMeme shows that clean, cold water is a precious resource and a symbol of the region's cherished rural way of life and independence.

rative power analysis to the campaign. It was clear that Nestlé had targeted McCloud because of its history as a former company town. It was once home to "Mother McCloud," a timber company whose mill was the heart of the town until it closed some 25 years ago. POW realized that Nestlé was tapping into a nostalgic narrative of the "good old days." The company presented themselves as Father Nestlé who would save the town by providing jobs and tax revenue. One local resident described how Nestlé's representative even tried to build rapport with locals by mimicking McCloud fashion, exchanging his business suits for jeans and cowboy boots.

As the campaign heated up, Nestlé used many of the common divide-and-conquer tactics that big corporations often use to derail local opposition. They worked to frame the issue around the **control meme** of *jobs versus the environment*. They cast opponents of the plant as "out-of-towners" and "second-home owners" who were obstructing the "economic progress and development" the town desperately needed. They dismissed local concerns about large-scale water extraction as coming from "unreasonable environmentalists" who were more concerned about fish than jobs.

Nestlé had a signed contract with the town and seemingly immovable support from the pro-development County Board of Supervisors, but the concerned local residents did not give up. The coalition continued organizing and building

94

alliances, and with help from *smart*Meme, effectively won the **battle of the story.** They **framed** their campaign around water as a precious resource, both economically and as a symbol of the local way of life. They challenged Nestlé's There-Is-No-Alternative-Framing (see Section 3.8) by releasing their own economic report, which revealed that the plant would offer only low-wage jobs while dramatically increasing local truck traffic on the area's only two-lane highway. They showed how Nestlé's contract was a bad deal for the town. They **foreshadowed** a more hopeful vision of the town uniting around a fair development project that would protect the local ecosystem.

This ad created by smartMeme launched the Nestlé spurge meme and helped alert the broader community to the potential threat of Nestlé's proposed plant.

A key strategy was to expand the frame beyond the impacted people of McCloud to tell a story about the region-wide threats of unchecked water development. In particular, Protect Our Waters knew they had to reach the ranching community who were among the most influential groups in the county.

Nestlé's *jobs versus the environment* **framing** was designed to tap into the ranchers' history of contentious battles with environmentalists. It successfully kept the issue off the ranching communities' radar, but the threat to ranchers was real. Nestlé's proposed bottling plant was so large that it was clearly intended to be a first step toward further extraction of the county's ground water in additional locations.

In supporting the campaign, *smart*Meme worked to find a **meme** that could communicate the potential threat that Nestlé's bottling plant represented to the ranchers and the entire county. We experimented with **brand busting** and combined a humorous appropriation of Nestlé's signature striped straw from their flagship *Nestlé Quik* chocolate drink, with a threat that was already familiar to the ranchers: "the spurge." The spurge is

This is a victory not just for the people of McCloud and their local ecosystem but for people everywhere who are standing up to corporate water privatizers.

an invasive plant species that degrades ranch land by absorbing too much water.

A double entendre was born—the Nestlé Spurge—a new type of invasive plant that also degrades the land by sucking up too much water. The campaign printed up materials modeled on pre-existing invasive plant alerts (playing with the cultural expressions of signage in the area). POW launched the **meme** at the biggest community event of the year: the County Fair.

Nestlé had also set up an informational table at the event. By all accounts, Nestlé's representatives heard from numerous county residents who were starting to see Nestlé as a bad neighbor and the proposed plant as the first step in a full-scale water grab. The spurge **meme** experiment had proved successful!

The tireless activists of the Protect Our Waters coalition continued their efforts. In August of 2008 they won a major victory when Nestlé agreed to renegotiate the contract it had signed with the town. For the next year the community explored options that would minimize environmental damage and insure real economic benefits to the town. In September of 2009, nearly 6 years after Nestlé's intentions became public, the company announced that it was abandoning its plans and leaving McCloud for good. This is a victory not just for the people of McCloud and their local ecosystem but for people everywhere who are standing up to corporate water privatizers.

5.5 CASE STUDY
The Coalition of Immokalee Workers:
Consciousness + Commitment = Change

One of the most inspiring contemporary U.S. organizing efforts is the work of The Coalition of Immokalee Workers (CIW) to build power and improve conditions for tomato pickers in southwestern Florida.[5] Immokalee is the state's largest farmworker community and is composed mostly of immigrants from Mexico (50%), Guatemala (30%), and Haiti (10%) as well as African Americans.[6] Poverty wages, abuse of workers, and even literal enslavement are common. CIW "strives to build strength as a community on a basis of reflection and analysis, constant attention to coalition building across ethnic divisions, and an ongoing investment in leadership development to help our members continually develop their skills in community education and organization."[7]

Re:Imagining Change

CIW began organizing in 1993 as a small group of workers meeting in an Immokalee church. In the 1990s, they took action at the **point of production**, including three general strikes, and built public pressure on tomato growers with marches, hunger strikes, and other tactics. From 1997 to 2001, CIW helped expose three modern-day slavery operations and freed 500 workers from indentured servitude. These efforts won better conditions in the tomato industry, and built more power for CIW.

But with their power analysis, they knew that in order to change the tomato industry, they had to go further up the food chain. So, they set their sights on changing the purchasing practices of the fast-food companies that buy the tomatoes wholesale.

In 2001, CIW launched the national boycott of Taco Bell—calling on the fast-food giant to take responsibility for human rights abuses in the fields. They demanded that Taco Bell pay one penny more per pound of tomatoes in order to give farmworkers a fairer wage for their labor. CIW also proposed an enforceable human rights code of conduct that includes farmworkers in monitoring working

The Coalition of Immokalee Workers have brought the struggle of tomato pickers—some of the poorest and most marginalized workers in the country—to the point of consumption in the fast-food industry. Their inspiring campaigns have won wage increases for farmworkers and enforceable human rights agreements with tomato purchasers like Taco Bell, McDonald's, Burger King, and Whole Foods.

conditions and holding companies accountable for sourcing tomatoes from sweatshop operations.

The Taco Bell boycott gained broad student, religious, labor, and community support in the nearly four years of its campaign. Boycott committees operated in nearly all 50 states. One of the most vibrant aspects of the campaign was the Student/ Farmworker Alliance (SFA) who led a fast-growing movement to "Boot the Bell" from college and high school campuses across the country.[8]

The campaign amplified the voices of workers telling their stories about life in Immokalee. The core meme of their demand was: "One more penny per pound!" The framing of the boycott around slavery targeted assumptions about working conditions and made the invisible visible.

SFA operates as an ally to CIW, organizing students and youth across the country. Since Taco Bell's marketing targeted young people, this was a key constituency on the campaign power map. Working with CIW, SFA creatively engaged in **brand busting** tactics like appropriating Taco Bell's chihuahua dog mascot and slogan to say "Yo No Quiero Taco Bell," and subverting the company's omnipresent "Think Outside the Bun" tagline to become "Think Outside the Bell!" They supported the boycott with actions at the **point of consumption,** at chain stores on and off campuses.

Large-scale national actions at the **point of decision** included a 10-day hunger strike outside of Taco Bell headquarters in Irvine, CA. This was one of the largest hunger strikes in U.S. labor history, with over 75 farmworkers and students fasting during the 10-day period in 2003. In 2004 and 2005, the Taco Bell Truth Tours went cross-country featuring marches and actions at the corporate headquarters of Yum! Brands (Taco Bell's parent company) in Louisville, Kentucky.

All the while the CIW was telling their story with dramatic imagery: pyramids of the tomato picking buckets representing the amount of tomatoes in a day's work, photo galleries of workers' calloused hands, colorful giant puppets of tomatoes and the Taco Bell chihuahua. The campaign amplified the voices of workers telling their stories about life in Immokalee. The core **meme** of their demand was: "One more penny per pound!" The **framing** of the boycott around slavery targeted **assumptions** about working conditions and made the invisible visible. The CIW

Re:Imagining Change

exposed human trafficking and bondage in the United States, a practice most people thought was long gone.

In March of 2005, on the eve of a major national convergence at their headquarters, Taco Bell's parent company Yum! Brands signed an agreement to meet the CIW's demands. Since that time, the Coalition of Immokalee Workers has successfully targeted McDonald's and Burger King with the model of the Taco Bell campaign, and has won! They are also advancing on the grocery industry and have pressured Whole Foods to adopt a similar purchasing and human rights policy.

The Student/Farmworker Alliance creatively engaged in brand busting tactics like appropriating Taco Bell's Chihuahua dog mascot and subverting the company's omnipresent "Think Outside the Bun" tagline to become "Think Outside the Bell!"

The CIW's successful alliance building within Immokalee, and with student and faith communities nationally, has built a powerful movement for justice. In 2006, they launched the Alliance for Fair Food network to build power for human rights throughout the U.S. food system.[9] Their local efforts in Immokalee include a radio station, community center, ongoing popular education, and exposing slavery and human rights violations. They also support cultural work in the community, and help build cooperatives of growers who pay fair wages.

The CIW's core philosophy is "consciousness + commitment = change" and they prove it to be true! The Coalition is truly an inspirational challenge to corporate power, and an instructive model for the kind of work our world so urgently needs.[10]

It's about a fight for the planet's resources, but the fight is taking place through a capture of the mind. We can only liberate our rivers and our seeds and our food, and our educational systems, and redefine and deepen our democracy, by first liberating our minds and decolonizing our minds.

~ Vandana Shiva[1]

6. Facing the Ecological Crisis: A Call to Innovation

6.1 Beyond Talking Points

> Frames emerge from history, and they are connected with institutions. To win, we must take on all of it—the frames, the history, and the institutions. We must have the courage to name what is right and plot a course that connects to everyday lives and transforms them. If we do this, we can re-frame our movements in ways that astonish, delight, and liberate.
> ~ From *The Soul of Environmentalism*, a response to *The Death of Environmentalism* by environmental justice leaders[2]

Tune in to any serious scientific or long-term policy discussion and you can't avoid the symptoms—mass extinction, global warming destabilizing the climate, skyrocketing disease rates linked to pollution, and the depletion of key resources such as topsoil, fresh water, biodiversity, and cheap oil.

These converging trends suggest a troubling forecast for our future. The ecological crisis is already feeding the historic dynamics of militarism, entrenched corporate power, and the systems of racism and oppression that have haunted the human family for generations. It is tragically predictable that the impacts of environmental collapse—like all structural problems— will follow the well-worn tracks of privilege that divide haves from have-nots.

The worst scenarios are rarely discussed but increasingly foreshadowed: private mercenary armies on the flooded streets of post-Katrina New Orleans. The militarized water grabs in the West Bank. Financial meltdown and global recession. Food riots.

More wars over the planet's remaining oil supplies...This version of our future is already all too familiar.

It is inaccurate to compartmentalize these overlapping crises as an "environmental issue," or an "energy issue," or any type of "single issue." Rather they are warning signs that our global system—which is based on centuries of unchecked industrial expansion, colonial conquest, and exploitation—has brought our planet's ecological life-support systems perilously close to collapse. The crisis is the (often unacknowledged) white noise behind all discussions about the future—the future for our children, for our communities, for the economy, for the role of government, and for global society as a whole.

Hurricane Ike hits Galveston, Texas, in September 2008. The hurricane killed 114 people in Haiti, Cuba, and the U.S. and is estimated to have caused over $10 billion worth of damage.

*Smart*Meme's roots are in the **earth-centered** politics of ecological resistance movements. We founded the organization and wrote *Re:Imagining Change* because we believe that our lifetimes come at a decisive moment in the history of our planet—a moment that requires creative, bold, and strategic action.

Our times call out for more powerful and effective social movements. We need not only bigger movements but also better strategies to confront the crises head on. We need to unearth the deep roots of our social and ecological problems in the worldview of the **dominant culture**. Social change, at the sweeping scale we need, will require systematic intervention into the pathological assumptions and **control mythologies** that maintain the status quo and limit the collective imagination of alternatives. Our movements need to

It is tragically predictable that the impacts of environmental collapse—like all structural problems— will follow the well-worn tracks of privilege that divide haves from have-nots.

Re:Imagining Change

go beyond talking points and isolated policy proposals to actually shift the narratives that shape popular understanding of our economy, our political system, and our entire relationship with the natural world.

6.2 The Slow-Motion Apocalypse

> We're in a giant car heading towards a brick wall and everyone's arguing over where they're going to sit.
> ~ David Suzuki

Our lifetimes are witness to a *slow-motion apocalypse*—the gradual unraveling of the routines, expectations and institutions that comfort the privileged, and define the status quo.

But the word apocalypse does not mean the end of the world. The Greek word *apokalypsis* combines the verb "kalypto," meaning "to cover or to hide," with the prefix "apo," meaning "away." *Apocalypse* literally means to "take the cover away," or to "lift the veil" and reveal something that has not been seen.[3]

The militarized streets of New Orleans in the wake of Hurricane Katrina (September 2005)

And thus these are indeed apocalyptic times. A 2008 poll reveals that 62% of Americans already agree with the statement "The earth is headed for an environmental catastrophe unless we change."[4] As the veil lifts, the assumptions and narratives that rationalize the status quo are shifting. What has been made invisible (by propaganda and privilege alike) has become a glaring truth: global corporate capitalism is on a collision course with the planet's ecological limits.

As activists, we often dare not speak this whole truth for

Indigenous women march in Mexico City at the Fourth World Water Forum to demand that water be recognized as a human right (March 2006). Photo by Orin Langelle.

fear of self-marginalizing, terrifying people, or worse—dousing the essential fires of hope with a paralyzing despair.

Indeed, to face the scale and implications of the ecological crisis requires a degree of psychological courage. The lifting of the veil can release an emotional rollercoaster of anxiety, anger, grief, and despair. When we take it all in—all of the suffering, all of the destruction, all that is at risk—added onto our ongoing daily struggles, it is difficult not to be overwhelmed. Denial is a common response and an effective poultice, however temporary.

A **narrative power analysis** helps us understand denial as a dynamic that shapes the terms of the debate around the ecological crisis. The assumption that the United States can "go green" on its current path, rather than fundamentally change our systems to operate within ecological limits, is one such manifestation. Denial is one of the key psychological undercurrents in the **dominant culture** that is preventing widespread acknowledgement of the scope of the ecological crisis, and keeping the apocalypse suspended in surreal slow motion. Denial is a more comfortable alternative to despair, but its impact on the collective political imagination is equally corrosive.

> *We believe that our lifetimes come at a decisive moment in the history of our planet—a moment that requires creative, bold, and strategic action.*

We also see this dynamic inside of progressive movements. Among many dedicated activist groups, there is an unstated culture of self-preserving denial. We see it expressed in various ways: rigid boundaries around an issue or constituency, an exclusive focus on short-term "wins," and a suspension of disbelief about the limits of current strategies to face the crisis. The underlying assumption is that *if we just keep doing what we've been doing, and just work harder at it, it will be enough.*

Stagnation is the prevailing creative tendency in too many of our organizations. While some tactics are improved, innovation of strategies is perennially postponed. The undertow of denial can keep our movements trapped in a crisis of imagination. The consequences are a policy paradigm incapable of dealing with the scope of the overlapping crises. The sector plods on while an increasingly unnerved public is left vulnerable to fear-mongering, corporate greenwashing, and phony quick-fix techno solutions.

6.3 Psychic Breaks

> Sometimes a breakdown can be the beginning of a kind of break-
> through, a way of living in advance through a trauma that prepares
> you for a future of radical transformation.
> ~ Cherríe Moraga

But what happens when denial is shattered by unfolding events?
Dramatic crisis situations can challenge underlying assumptions
and redefine the conventional wisdom.
These cultural and political moments
freeze-frame and expose the limitations
of current understandings: 9/11, the U.S.
invasion of Iraq, the flooding of New Orleans, and the 2008 Wall Street meltdown are all recent examples.

These sorts of seismic events inevitably disrupt the dominant culture's
mental maps and can trigger mass **psychic breaks**: moments when status quo
stories no longer hold true, and a critical
mass of people can't deny that what is
happening in the world is out of alignment with their values. People are left
searching for new explanations, and are
potentially open to new perspectives and
willing to take new risks. As a result, the
narrative landscape can shift rapidly and
unexpectedly as the terms of debate are
redefined.

Psychic breaks can occur when the conventional wisdom is shattered by unfolding events. The 2008 financial meltdown on Wall Street led many people to question the system, and changed the conversation about regulation and the free-market ideology.

Psychic breaks open new political
space and can provide powerful opportu-
nities for new stories to take root in popular consciousness. We've
seen it in the upwelling of community building since 9/11, the
outrage and mass civil disobedience during the U.S. military invasion of Iraq, the outpouring of mutual aid during hurricane Katrina, and the fallout from the Wall Street financial meltdown and
the contested story of free-market ideology.

Unfortunately, though, these moments are often hijacked by
power-holders who use fear to manipulate trauma and re-en-
trench old power dynamics. The post-9/11 **psychic break** quickly

turned to warmongering, hate crimes against Muslim Americans, and the swift passage of the PATRIOT Act. The Iraq invasion was accompanied with feverish, bloodthirsty rhetoric couched as patriotism. The historic election of Barack Obama also sparked a right-wing backlash that has used thinly veiled racism to attack his agenda and slow reforms. In the absence of effective progressive framing, the 2008-09 financial crisis was packaged with fear-mongering memes like "Too Big to Fail," "Meltdown," and "Great Depression" to pass a multi-trillion dollar bailout that mainly benefited the largest companies and super-rich investors.

Seismic events can trigger mass psychic breaks: moments when status quo stories no longer hold true, and a critical mass of people can't deny that what is happening in the world is out of alignment with their values.

As we see more eco-spasms, resource grabs, economic disruptions and mass displacement, the myths that glue the system together will strain under pressure and more people will experience **psychic breaks**. While right wing mouthpieces like Fox News fan the flames of discontent with the racism of the "Tea Party" narrative, our movements are failing to offer accessible narratives and frame popular understanding of the complicated crises that define our times. As the crisis compounds, these events have a momentum of their own—with or without us.

As the slow-motion apocalypse accelerates, will the fallout trigger more reactionary backlash or true progressive change? Will the mass **psychic breaks** of the future unleash popular momentum for social transformation? Or will they serve as an excuse for mass manipulation by desperate elites struggling to maintain the status quo?

The answers depend on how effectively **change agents** can harness awakenings from denial to build movements that can fundamentally shift the course of events. As the **control mythologies** unravel, our movements can offer new narratives and foreshadow new, more just futures...but to do so means we must be ready to wage the **battle of story** in the midst of upheaval, fracture, and rapid change. In this day and age, where cascading events unfold in the 24-hour media environment, when the old story is eroding rapidly, we have to be ready to intervene in the spectacle, **reframe**, and launch new stories.

Re:Imagining Change

6.4 Toward Ecological Justice

There are no passengers on Spaceship Earth. We are all crew.
~ Marshall McLuhan

The history of grassroots social change teaches, "the whole is greater than the sum of its parts." This equation reflects the power of narrative to multiply a social movement's power when a common story unites and mobilizes popular energy toward shared goals.

We must be willing to take risks and re-imagine not only a vision for our communities, but also a vision of what social change process and practice can look like.

At *smart*Meme, we believe that our times demand that we build more holistic movements with the capacity to tell stories that bring together a commitment to social justice with the vision of an ecologically sane future. We believe that to address the global challenges of our lifetimes, our movements must cultivate a broader understanding of **narrative power** and develop more sophisticated **story-based strategies**. Our movements need to nurture a culture of strategic innovation. Organizations need Research and Development budgets, street level laboratories, and a swarm of creative strategists. We need to shift the activist culture to see innovation not as a luxury at the edge of "the work," but rather as a necessity at the heart of "the work." We must be willing to take risks and re-imagine not only a vision for our communities, but also a vision of what social change process and practice can look like.

And make no mistake, bold innovations are afoot: From the community supported agriculture

Representatives from the Indigenous Peoples Caucus lead a march of over 100,000 people outside the United Nations COP-15 climate summit in Copenhagen. The mobilization brought together an alliance of global movements taking action both inside and outside the conference to demand "system change not climate change." (December 2009) Photo by Orin Langelle/GJEP-GFC

Innovators at the Movement Generation Justice & Ecology Project are redefining the potential of earth-centered politics by "cultivating an urban justice based approach to ecology." (www.movementgeneration.org)

(CSA) program of the Milwaukee racial justice organization Growing Power, to the cross-cutting work at the Center for Media Justice in Oakland, to the community-based corporate campaigning of the Coalition of Immokalee Workers (CIW) in Florida. There are countless examples of cross-sector work bubbling up in communities across the country. Innovative organizations are stepping beyond single-issue politics to open new political spaces, test new models and embrace new organizational forms. Leaders are forging new alliances that build unity amongst different issues, constituencies, and movements without creating structures that deny our differences or compromise our diversity. The victory of the Obama campaign showed the power of hopeful stories to unite people, and the mobilizing potential of the Millennial generation, who mashed up Twittering and good old-fashioned door-knocking to get out the vote in record numbers.

The transformational stories of 21st-century change will celebrate the heroes at the margins, inspire us to face the true scale of our problems, and herald visions of a world remade.

Now the Obama presidency (and resulting backlash) has complicated how social movements engage around numerous issues and underscored the need for flexibility and innovation.

In the midst of this historic moment, one of the exciting trends is the growing momentum linking ecological politics with social justice organizing. Around the world, the call for "climate justice" is galvanizing social movements to address the root causes of the climate crisis. In the U.S., trailblazing groups like the Movement Generation Justice & Ecology Project are designing political education curricula and facilitating strategic planning for action around the ecological crisis for economic and racial justice organizers working in urban communi-

Re:Imagining Change is a call to innovation and a call to action. Join with smartMeme to change the story for a better future.

ties of color.

New ways of telling our stories that combine ecological analysis with the historic demands for equity and justice are emerging. Memes like "just transition" and "**ecological justice**" are spreading and challenging status quo assumptions. Visions are taking shape, foreshadowing the multi-racial alliances, networks and grassroots movements that will undertake the grand project of redesigning our society to be both sustainable and inclusive. Collectively the work to craft a politics that is commensurate with the scale of the crisis is evolving.

Story-based strategy has an important role to play in supporting these types of innovations. When we come together across social divides to share our histories and our dreams, new understandings of interconnection can emerge. Storytelling can help us build relationship across divides of race, class, gender, and culture. **Story-based strategy** can help us articulate shared values and more effectively communicate the connections between all the "issues."

The name *smart*Meme is inspired by a vision of grassroots **change agents** collaboratively creating and unleashing **memes** designed to challenge assumptions and change destructive stories. The *smart* implies both effective and networked: **memes** that are born from and spread through **people-powered** collaboration. Our movements desperately need smart*er* memes that encapsulate and popularize stories with the creative power to point us toward a more democratic, just, peaceful, and ecologically sane future.

*Smart*Meme's years of experimentation lead us to believe that there is vast transformative potential in narrative social change strategies. The **story-based strategy** model that we've outlined in the preceding pages is a rudimentary sketch of the possibilities. There are more ideas to explore, more stories to tell, and more interventions to imagine. We offer *Re:Imagining Change* as an invitation to **change agents** from all walks of life to embrace a vision of **ecological justice**, and step into your power as strategists and storytellers.

To succeed we must resist the despair and overcome the denial that have shaped our responses to the crisis for too long. Our generations have the opportunity to lead a path toward ecological reconstruction, mass reconciliation, a more free, just society, and ultimately a better world for all.

But to succeed our movements must become the culture's storytellers. The transformational stories of 21st-century change will applaud the heroes at the margins, inspire us to face the true scale of our problems, and herald visions of a world remade. They will accommodate complexity, celebrate diversity, and foreshadow the challenges and triumphs we all will face. But these stories will not be handed down from the **meme**-makers on high. They will emerge as collaborative strategies from communities and grassroots movements. They will emerge from struggle and celebration.

Our movements can transform fear and denial into hope and action, if we have the courage to experiment, innovate, struggle, and win. In the new stories emerging from grassroots movements around the planet lie the creative sparks to reimagine change and remake our world.

Endnotes

I. Introduction: The Power of Stories

1. A very useful exploration of these issues and a call for progressives to create "ethical spectacles" can be found in Stephen Duncombe's book *Dream: Re-Imagining Progressive Politics in the Age of Fantasy* (The New Press, 2007).

2. Please see *smart*Meme's Anti-Oppression Principles at www.smart-meme.org.

3. See tools and training at: http://www.trainingforchange.org and http://www.ruckus.org.

4. See tools and training at: http://www.spinproject.org.

5. Check out the National Organizers Alliance: http://www.noacentral.org.

6. Check out the Catalyst Project's great summary of antiracism training resources: http://www.collectiveliberation.org.

II. Narrative Power Analysis

1. From "The Secrets of Storytelling: Why we love a good yarn," *Scientific American,* September 18, 2008. We got this link from our friends at the Pop-Anthropology blog (http://www.thirsty-fish.com/popanthroblog/).

2. Ibid.

3. From http://www.wordnet.princeton.edu. The pejorative usage of a "myth-as-lie" often dismisses the deeper relevance of "myth-as-meaning."

4. We were introduced to this exercise by Sha'an Mouliert in her anti-oppression training at the 2005 *smart*Meme national gathering in-cite/insight.

5. Narrative has always been a human obsession and there are many different theories and approaches to exploring the issue. Each of these terms brings its own discourse and analytical tools to the discussion. For some very useful insights into cosmology—literally the story of the universe–and thinking on how to change these stories, check out the work of Thomas Berry. Likewise, Joseph Campbell's very accessible work is a good starting point on myth. The term metanarrative was originally coined in the 1970's by French philosopher and critic Jean-François Lyotard (who declared its death) and has become a staple of post-modern thought.

6. The essence of Sharp's theory of power is quite simple: people in society may be divided into rulers and subjects; the power of rulers derives from consent by the subjects; systematic nonviolent action is a process of withdrawing consent and thus is a way to challenge the key modern problems of dictatorship, genocide, war, and systems of oppression. Gene Sharp's book, *The Politics of Nonviolent Action* (1973), is widely regarded as a classic. Other important works by Sharp are two collections of essays, *Social Power and Political Freedom* (1980) and *Gandhi as a Political Strategist* (1979). There are numerous critiques of Sharp's work, and of his Albert Einstein Institution's consulting practice, particularly in Venezuela. However, it is widely understood that Sharp's work is a major contribution to 20th-century social movement theory. *Smart*Meme owes great intellectual debt to Jethro Heiko and Nick Jehlen of the Action Mill for their efforts to integrate the applications of this theory drawn from the Serbian student movement *Otpor* and their "upside-down triangle" curriculum into a U.S. context. *Smart*Meme has supported Action Mill in applying this framework with Iraq Veterans Against the War, who use the consent theory as the core of their antiwar strategy (http://ivaw.org/publicdocuments/strategypamphlet.pdf).

7 Check out wikipedia for some useful notes on Gramsci: http://en.wikipedia.org/wiki/Antonio_Gramsci. The original writings are compiled in his *Prison Notebooks*.

8. For another side of the story of Thanksgiving see the Bureau of White Affairs http://www.unitednativeamerica.com/bureau/bwa_2.html and United American Indians of New England: http://www.uaine.org.

9. The phrase was first coined by 19th-century German philosopher Friedrich Nietzsche and expanded upon by Walter Benjamin, now it is a meme with a life of its own and has largely been accepted as conventional wisdom.

10. For information on ongoing organizing and protest see United American Indians of New England: http://www.uaine.org.

11. Drew Weston's *Political Brain* (Public Affairs, 2007) examines the biological roots of partisanship and provides superb examples of the power of messaging.

12. This stat is a hybrid estimate from several sources including projections by PricewaterhouseCoopers, Plunkett Research and Advertising Age magazine.

13. www.plunkettresearch.com

14. From the Federal Trade Commission (2007) http://www.ftc.gov/os/2007/06/cabecolor.pdf.

15. Paul M. Fischer et al, "Brand logo recognition by children aged 3 to 6 years: Mickey Mouse and Old Joe the Camel," Journal of the American Medical Association 266 (11 Dec. 1991): 3145-48.

16. From the National Institute on Media & The Family based on George Comstock's *Television and the American Child* (Academic Press Inc. 1991) & James McNeal's *Kids as Customers* (Lexington Books, 1992) Compiled stats available at http://www.mediafamily.org/facts/facts_childadv.shtml

17. Check out any of Sut Jhally's prolific and influential writing and multimedia output. A particular favorite is his essay and video lecture *Advertising and the End of the World*. The work of Jhally and many other important cultural critics can be found at the Media Education Foundation: http://www.mediaed.org.

18. See Dumcombe's book, *Dream: Re-Imagining Progressive Politics in an Age of Fantasy* (The New Press, 2007).

19. Allen, Frederick: *Secret Formula: How Brilliant Marketing and Relentless Salesmanship Made Coca-Cola the Best Known Product in the World.* (Harper Collins, 1995) p. 207

20. Silverstein, Barry, "A Few Brand Campaigns Are Forever (Well, Almost)," Published on *MarketingProfs.com* on January 17, 2006 (http://www.marketingprofs.com/6/silverstein2.asp?part=2).

21. The origins of branding were drawn to our attention by our colleague Sean A. Witters who explores the issue in his forthcoming book, *Literary Authenticity: Authorship and the Logic of the Brand in the Modern American Novel*

22. The corporate alphabet was created by Heidi Cody (http://www.heidicody.com) and used by Carrie McLaren and *Stay Free* Magazine in their High School Media Literacy Curriculum http://www.stayfreemagazine.org/ml/index.html.

23. "Memes: Introduction," by Glenn Grant, Memeticist http://pespmc1.vub.ac.be/MEMIN.html.

24. Ibid.

25. See the insightful commentary regarding memes in the 2008 election cycle, "I'm Rubber, You're Glue," by Jonathan Alter in *Newsweek* September 1, 2008 http://www.newsweek.com/id/155115/page/1.

26. The terms Internalized Racial Superiority and Internalized Racial Inferiority come from the antiracism principles of the Peoples Institute for Survival and Beyond: http://www.pisab.org.

27. Polleta, Francesca *It was Like a Fever: Storytelling in Protest and Politics* (University of Chicago Press, 2006) an excellent resource for examining the complexity of social movement applications of storytelling.

III. Winning the Battle of the Story

1. For a chilling look at the PR industry's practices see the classic *Toxic Sludge is Good For You: Lies, Damn Lies, and the Public Relations Industry.* John Stauber and Sheldon Rampton (Common Courage Press, 1995).

2. We first encountered the term Battle of the Story in the work of the RAND Corporation, a wide-ranging private think tank specializing in military and corporate research. The term was used by RAND analysts John Arquilla and David Ronfeldt who co-wrote *Networks and Networks: The Future of Terror, Crime, and Militancy* (RAND, 2001).

3. Lakoff is a cognitive linguist, professor at UC Berkeley and co-founder of the now shuttered Rockridge Institute (www.rockridgeinstitute.org). He is the author of numerous books, including *Don't Think of an Elephant* (Chelsea Green, 2004) and *Whose Freedom?* (Farrar, Straus and Giroux, 2006). On framing, see also: "The Framing Wars" from 2005 *New York Times Magazine*:
http://www.nytimes.com/2005/07/17/magazine/17DEMOCRATS.html?_r=1&pagewanted=1&ei=5070&en=e3e686efd4fa97c5&ex=1183608000&oref=slogin.

4. Goffman, Erving *Frame Analysis: An essay on the organization of experience.* Pg 21 (Harvard University Press, 1974).

5. Quote reported in "Snap Judgments: Did Iconic Images from Baghdad Reveal More About the Media than Iraq?" by Matthew Gilbert and Suzanne Ryan April 10, 2003 Boston Globe Pg D1. Available at:
http://www.boston.com/news/packages/iraq/globe_stories/041003_snap_judgements.htm.

6. "Baghdad: the Day After" by Robert Fisk U.K. *Independent* April 11, 2003 available at:
www.independent.co.uk/opinion/commentators/fisk/robert-fisk-baghdad-the-day-after-594104.html.

7. This aspect of the ongoing story of the Pentagon's efforts to manipulate U.S. media coverage of the war was broken in a major multi-page

exposé by the *New York Times* "Behind TV Analysts, Pentagon's Hidden Hand" by David Barstow April 20, 2008.

8. For a deeper exploration of information warfare and the dynamics of its use against nonviolent protest movements check out smart-Meme's analysis of protests at the 2003 Free Trade Area of the Americas Summit in Miami. The article "Information Warfare in Miami" can be found at http://www.smartMeme.org.

9. http://www.mfso.org.

10. http://www.ivaw.org.

11. Stacey Malkan's *Not Just a Pretty Face: The Ugly Side of the Beauty Industry* (New Society Publishers, 2007) is an excellent book from a frontline environmental health activist and researcher. Also see the Environmental Working Group's 2005 Report Skin Deep and their updated product safety database at http://www.cosmeticdatabase.com.

12. http://www.safecosmetics.org.

13. Lasn, Kalle *Culture Jam: How to Reverse America's Suicidal Consumer Binge—and Why We Must* (HarperCollins, 1999). Also check out Adbuster magazine at http://www.adbusters.org.

14. For more analysis on the Capitol Climate Action, see http://smart-meme.org/blog/?p=39.

15. The term "meme campaigning," as far as we know, was coined by long time creative activist and agitator Andrew Boyd. Andrew, charming and humble man that he is, put it this way: "You can call me a co-coiner of the phrase along with a host of others in the secret people's history of viral organizing." We love that guy. Check out his latest projects at http://www.agit-pop.com and http://www.wanderbody.com. .

16. See The Rand Corporation's whitepaper *What Next for Networks and Netwars?* http://www.rand.org/pubs/monograph_reports/MR1382/MR1382.ch10.pdf.

17. For a excellent description and analysis of the campaign, read Billionaires co-founder Andrew Boyd's essay "Truth is a Virus: Meme Warfare and the Billionaires for Bush (or Gore)" published in the *Cultural Resistance Reader* edited by Stephen Duncombe (Verso, 2002).

IV. Points of Intervention

1. To see the "market campaign" model in action, check out the work of the Rainforest Action Network (http://www.ran.org) or ForestEthics (http://www.forestethics.org). For a good inventory of the model being used in different sectors see http://www.businessethicsnetwork.org, and check out *Insurrection: The Citizen Challenge to Corporate Power* by Kevin Danaher and Jason Mark (Routledge, 2003).

2. This process of a collective acceptance of a common narrative is sometimes called *"frame alignment"*. For useful concepts for frame analysis see: http://www.ccsr.ac.uk/methods/publications/frame-analysis/framing_concepts.html—this is a summary of the discourse including the foundational work of Snow & Benford. "Ideology, Frame Resonance and Participant Mobilization," *International Social Movement Research* 1:197-219. (1988).

3. TINA—there is no alternative—is a phrase coined by British Prime Minister Margaret Thatcher in the early 1980s as part of her austerity campaign of shredding the British welfare system, instituting mass privatization, and challenging organized labor. Her economic policies become a model for much of the neoliberal reforms that have now became tragically common around the world.

4. This action is well documented in a number of histories of the U.S. radical ecology movement and described in Martha F. Lee's *Earth First! Environmental Apocalypse* (Syracuse University Press, 1995).

5. http://www.turnyourbackonbush.org.

V. Changing the Story

1. See Rex Weyler's *Greenpeace: The Inside Story* (Rodale, 2005).

2. For a video clip of the save the whales campaign, see: http://archives.cbc.ca/IDC-1-69-867 5005/life_society/greenpeace/clip3.

3. See the campaign archive at: http://www.ruralvermont.org/gmos.html.

4. For more information about the destructive nature of the bottled water industry see www.thinkoutsidethebottle.org.

5. See: http://ciw-online.org .

6. http://www.ciw-online.org/about.html.

7. Ibid.

8. SFA was *smart*Meme's first partner in our STORY youth program.

*Smart*Meme regards SFA as an exemplary model of an effective network of youth leaders working in accountable relationship with a directly impacted community in a worker-led alliance. The SFA operates in a youth-led model of mobilizing students through a corporate campaign, which is led by people who are most directly affected in the corporate race-to-the-bottom. *Smart*Meme has supported SFA in developing their message and media capacity, as well as their overall story and visual brand. *Smart*Meme also supported leadership development work by facilitating strategy sessions and offering story-based strategy trainings at the (now annual) "Youth Encuentro in Immokalee." Visit them @ http://www.sfalliance.org.

9. http://www.allianceforfairfood.org.

10. See David Solnit's 2005 *Left Turn* article "Taco Bell Boycott Victory—A Model of Strategic Organizing: An interview with the Coalition of Immokalee Workers": http://www.leftturn.org/?q=node/335.

VI. Afterword

1. From "The River vs. Water, Inc: An interview with Vandana Shiva" by Antonia Juhasz for *LiP Magazine* (October 28, 2005) http://www.lipmagazine.org/articles/featshiva_water.htm.

2. From "The Soul of Environmentalism: Rediscovering transformational politics in the 21st century" By Michel Gelobter, Michael Dorsey, Leslie Fields, Tom Goldtooth, Anuja Mendiratta, Richard Moore, Rachel Morello-Frosch, Peggy M. Shepard & Gerald Torres (May 27, 2005) http://www.rprogress.org/soul/soul.pdf.

3. Edinger, Edward F. *Archetype of the Apocalypse: Divine Vengeance, Terrorism, and the End of the World* 1999 Open Court: Chicago. Until his death in 1999 Edinger was one of the leading Jungian analysts in the U.S.

4. *A New Values Survey, on The Emerging Wisdom Culture and New Political Compass* by Paul H. Ray (Unpublished, 2008).

Glossary

action logic – the explicit or implicit narrative that is illustrated by a specific action; how an action makes sense politically to an outside observer (see **meta-verb**).

advertising – the manipulation of collective desire for commercial/political interests (see also **branding**).

apocalypse – the Greek word apokalypsis combines the verb "kalypto" meaning to "cover or to hide," with the prefix "apo" meaning "away." Apocalypse literally means to "take the cover away," or to "lift the veil" and reveal something that has not been seen.

assumption – something that is accepted as true without proof; hypothesis that is taken for granted.

battle of the story – 1. the political contest of defining meaning and framing a situation (or issue) for a popular audience 2. a social change narrative with the goal of persuading people who aren't necessarily already in agreement with the social change effort. (See also **story of the battle.**)

branding – the processes and demarcations to endow an object (product), idea, or person with specific narrative and emotional qualities. A common expression of narrative power and a cornerstone concept for the age of hyperconsumerism and corporatized culture.

brand busting – a tactic to pressure corporate decision makers by linking the company's public image or brand with the injustices they are perpetrating.

change agent – a person who embraces her or his own power as a catalyst; a term for anyone who is engaged in some form of **social change** work.

changing the story – a catch phrase to describe the complex process of shifting the dominant public understanding of an issue or situation.

confirmation bias – the concept emerging from psychological and cognitive studies on framing showing that people are more likely to believe new information if it resonates with their existing values or confirms things they already believe.

control meme – a meme that acts as a container for control myths or spreads oppressive stories. Commonly, a meme that marginalizes, co-opts, or limits the scale of social change ideas by institutionalizing a status quo bias into popular perception of events or ideas (e.g., separate-but-equal ... death tax, or surgical strike). (See also **meme.**)

control mythology – the web of stories, symbols, and ideas that define the dominant culture. Includes stories that assume the system is unchangeable or limit our imagination of social change.

culture – (from the Latin cultura stemming from colere, meaning "to cultivate") refers to patterns of human activity including ways of living, arts, beliefs, and institutions that are passed down through the generations. A matrix of shared mental maps that define collective meanings. (See also **narrative space**.)

culture jamming – a technique to subvert dominant culture narratives such as corporate advertising or control mythologies by co-opting slogans and images and re-contextualizing them to create (usually subversive) new meanings.

designer meme – a meme created for a specific purpose (See **smart meme** and **control meme**.)

dominant culture – the constellation of specific cultural beliefs, norms, and practices shaped by powerful interests that have been normalized (often as "mainstream") by marginalizing, invisiblizing, silencing, criminalizing, annihilating, or assimilating other cultural beliefs and practices through historical processes of domination and control. Sometimes also described as hegemony.

direct action at the point of assumption – action with the goal of intervention in narrative space in order to reframe social issues by targeting underlying assumptions and changing the story.

earth-centered – (1) a political perspective to situate your life and your efforts as a change agent in the context of the planet's ecological operating systems, cultural diversity, biodiversity, and efforts to re-center human society within the Earth's natural limits & cycles. (2) a politicized acceptance of the sacredness of living systems.

ecological justice – an emerging frame to describe holistic, community led responses to the ecological crisis that combine a vision of respect and restoration of natural systems with advocacy for justice in all its forms. (See **earth-centered**)

elements of story – the five components of a narrative that *smart*-Meme uses to apply a narrative power analysis: conflict, characters, images, foreshadowing, and underlying assumptions.

frame – the larger story that shapes understanding of information, experiences, and messages; the structure and boundaries of a narrative that defines point of view and power. Frames operate as pre-existing narrative lenses in our minds.

hegemony – a concept developed in the 1930s by the imprisoned Italian Communist leader Antonio Gramsci, describes how powerful interests and institutions don't just rule society with coercion and violence, but also define society's norms through a dominant culture. This multifaceted, intergenerational cultural process limits the terms of the debate to make ideas that challenge the status quo almost unthinkable.

information warfare – as defined by the U.S. military in the 1996 Chairman of the Joint Chiefs of Staff Instruction Number 3210.01: "Actions taken to achieve information superiority by affecting adversary information, information based processes, and information systems." It includes the realm of psychological operations and the manipulation of narrative and public opinion for military purposes.

intervention – an action meant to change the course of events; interference or interaction with a previously existing narrative, audience, social structure, system, venue or space.

meme – (rhymes with dream) a unit of self-replicating cultural information (e.g., idea, slogan, melody, ritual, symbol) that spreads virally from imagination to imagination and generation to generation. Coined by evolutionary biologist Richard Dawkins in 1976 as analogous to "gene," from a Greek root meaning "to imitate." Glenn Grant defines it as "A contagious information pattern." A meme operates as a container, capsule, or carrier for a story.

meta-verb – the overarching verb that embodies the narrative of a social action or intervention (e.g., resist, disrupt, counter, or expose). (See **action logic**.)

movement – a critical mass of people who share ideas and values, organize in large informal groupings and networks of individuals and/or organizations, take collective social action, and build alternative institutions to create social change.

narrative – *(from the Proto-Indo-European root gnō-, "to know")* a story or account of events, sequenced over time and space; a fundamental cognitive structuring process for the human mind to make meaning and relate with the world.

narrative filters – the existing stories and assumptions people have about the world that screen out new information that doesn't fit with their existing mental frame works (See **confirmation bias.**)

narrative logic – a coherent narrative structure that effectively communicates the desired message; all the elements of the story make sense together and reinforce the intended meaning. (See **action logic**)

narrative power – a multi-faceted and fluid form of power expressed through stories, particularly through the processes that socially construct specific stories as "the truth." (See **power** and **narrative power analysis.**)

narrative power analysis – an analytical framework for assessing the interactions between narrative and relationships of power. The approach is grounded in the recognition that since the human brain uses stories to understand the world, all power relations have a narrative dimension.

Re:Imagining Change

It can be used deconstructively to examine existing stories, as well as constructively to create new stories.

narrative space – the ethereal realm of common stories, ideas, and images that connect people in shared cultural and ideological frameworks.

narrowcasting – targeting information to a specific audience rather than the general public; the term emerged as a contrast to traditional broadcasting.

power-holder – an individual who possesses influence within a specific **power** structure. This person is sometimes known as a "decision maker," and is often the target of a campaign.

people-power – the term originates from the 1986 mass uprising when the people of the Philippines nonviolently overthrew their authoritarian government. It has come to mean any movement or social change strategy that recognizes that dominant institutions rely on the consent of the masses and that the removal of popular consent can lead to dramatic social changes.

point of intervention – a place in a system, be it a physical system or a conceptual system (ideology, cultural assumption, etc.) where action can be taken to effectively interfere with the system in order to change it. Examples include point of production (factory), point of destruction (logging road), point of consumption (retail store), point of decision (corporate headquarters), and point of assumption (intervening in an existing narrative, making alternatives visible).

popular culture – patterns of human activity and symbolic structures that are popular, often defined or determined by the mass media and expressed in vernacular language. The roots of the term relate to the culture of "the common people" in contrast with the "high culture" of elites.

power – a complex area of social change theory that we at *smart*Meme generally define as a dynamic set of relationships between people, institutions and ideas characterized by the (often unequal) distribution of controlling influence. We also use the "three-fold model" of power from strategic nonviolence—power over, power-with, and power within—as a way to name the types of power we are working with in social change endeavors. (See **narrative power**.)

psychic break – the process or moment of realization whereby a deeply held dominant culture narrative comes into question, oftentimes stemming from a revelation that a system, event, or course of events is out of alignment with core values.

racism – we find the definition provided by the People's Institute for Survival and Beyond to be particularly useful: "Racism is race prejudice plus power. Historically in the U.S. it has been the single most critical barrier to building effective coalitions for social change. Racism has been consciously and systematically erected, and it can be undone only if people understand what it is, where it comes from, how it functions, and why it is perpetuated."

radical – a problem-solving approach that focuses attention on addressing the root cause of problems rather than the symptoms. Also: a change agent who adopts this approach.

reframing – the process of shifting popular understanding of an issue, event or situation by changing the terms for how it is understood. (see **changing the story** and **frame**)

smart meme – a designer meme that aims to change the story by injecting ideas into popular culture, contesting established meaning (and/or control memes), and facilitating popular re-thinking of assumptions. Smart memes act as containers for collaborative power, reveal creative possibilities, and grow out of the networked possibility of grassroots social movements (compare with **control meme**).

social change – the holistic process of collectively changing social power relationships (and aspects therein) including processes, material conditions, institutional power and economic distribution—as well as narrative frameworks and culture.

spectacle – a concept coming from the work of the radical French artist-philosopher-revolutionary Guy Debord to describe "a social relation between people that is mediated by images."

story – a catch-all descriptor of all types of narratives, from mundane anecdotes to deep-seated cultural frameworks (See also **narrative** and **elements of story.**)

story-based strategy – a framework that links movement building with an analysis of narrative power and places storytelling at the center of social change strategy. The framework provides tools to craft more effective social change stories, challenge assumptions, intervene in prevailing cultural narratives, and **change the story** around an issue.

story of the battle – a social change narrative that intends to mobilize an audience of people who already share political assumptions with the communicator.

strategy – a premeditated and systematic plan of action to achieve a particular goal. Strategy is inseparable from analysis and requires reflection and flexibility to adapt to emergent situations.

Re:Imagining Change

Further Reading

Adams, Maurianne, Pat Griffin, and Lee A. Bell, eds. *Teaching for Diversity and Social Justice: A Sourcebook for Teachers and Trainers.* New York: Routledge, 1997.

Adamson, Joni, Mei M. Evans, and Rachel Stein, eds. *The Environmental Justice Reader: Politics, Poetics, and Pedagogy.* Tucson, AZ: University of Arizona Press, 2002.

Albert, Michael. *Parecon: Life after Capitalism.* New York: Verso Books, 2004.

Alinsky, Saul. *Rules for Radicals.* New York: Vintage, 1995.

Allen, Frederick. *Secret Formula: How Brilliant Marketing and Relentless Salesmanship Made Coca-Cola the Best Know Product in the World* New York: Harper Collins, 1995.

Allen, Theodore W. *The Invention of the White Race : Racial Oppression and Social Control.* New York: Verso Books, 1993.

Ancel, Judy, and Jane Slaughter. *A Troublemaker's Handbook 2: How to Fight Back Where You Work—and Win!* Lincoln: Labor Notes, 2005.

Arquilla, John, and David Ronfeldt *Networks and Netwars: The Future of Terror, Crime and Militancy.* RAND, 2001.

Aunger, Robert. *The Electric Meme.* New York: Free Press, 2002.

Berger, Dan. *Outlaws of America: The Weather Underground and the Politics of Solidarity.* Oakland, CA: AK Press, 2006.

Berry, Wendell, Daniel Kemmis, and Courtney White. *The Way of Ignorance: And Other Essays.* Berkeley, CA: Counterpoint, 2006.

Blackmore, Susan, *The Meme Machine.* Oxford [England]; New York Oxford University Press, 2000.

Boal, Augusto. *Theatre of the Oppressed.* New York: Theatre Communications Group, Incorporated, 1985.

Bookchin, Murray. *Post-Scarcity Anarchism.* New York: Penguin Group (USA) Incorporated, 2004.

——. *The Ecology of Freedom: The Emergence and Dissolution of Hierarchy.* Oakland, CA: AK Press, 2005.

Boyd, Herb. *Autobiography of a People: Three Centuries of African American History Told by Those Who Lived It.* New York: Anchor, 2000.

Bracken, Len. *Guy Debord: Revolutionary.* Venice, CA: Feral House 1997.

Brafman, Ori, and Rod A. Beckstrom. *The Starfish and the Spider: The Unstoppable Power of Leaderless Organizations.* New York: Portfolio (Hardcover), 2006.

Bray, Robert. *SPIN Works! A Media Guidebook for Communicating Values and Shaping Opinion.* San Francisco: Independent Media Institute, 2000.

Bringing Down a Dictator. Dir. Steve York. DVD. 2001-2002.

Brodie, Richard. *Virus of the Mind: The New Science of the Meme.* Seattle, WA: Integral Press, 2004.

Campbell, Joseph. *Myths to Live By.* New York: Bantam, 1984.

Century of the Self. Dir. Adam Curtis. DVD. 2007.

Chisom, Ronald, and Michael Washington. *Undoing Racism: A Philosophy of International Social Change.* 2nd ed. New Orleans, LA: Peoples' Institute Press, 1997.

Chomsky, Noam. *Media Control: The Spectacular Achievements of Propaganda.* New York: Seven Stories Press, 2004.

Claiborne, Shane, and Jim Wallis. *The Irresistible Revolution: Living as an Ordinary Radical.* Grand Rapids, MI: Zondervan, 2006.

Cockcroft, Eva, Cockcroft, Jim, and Weber, John. *Toward a People's Art.* New York: Dutton, 1977.

Collins, Chuck, and Felice Yeskel. *Economic Apartheid in America: A Primer on Economic Inequality and Insecurity.* New York: New Press, The, 2005.

Control Room. Dir. Jehane Noujaim. DVD. 2004.

Cutting, Hunter, and Makani Themba-Nixon, eds. *Talking the Walk : A Communications Guide for Racial Justice.* Oakland, CA: AK Press, 2006.

Danaher, Kevin, and Jason Mark. *Insurrection : Citizen Challenges to Corporate Power.* New York: Routledge, 2003.

Dawkins, Richard. *The Selfish Gene.*Oxford [England] ; New York: Oxford University Press, 2006.

Distin, Kate. *The Selfish Meme: A Critical Reassessment.* Cambridge, U.K. ; New York:Cambridge University Press, 2004.

Duncombe, Stephen. *Cultural Resistance: A Reader.* New York: Verso Books, 2002.

——. *Dream: Re-Imagining Progressive Politics in an Age of Fantasy.* New York: New Press, 2007.

During, Simon, ed. *The Cultural Studies Reader*. New York: Routledge, 1999.

Duvall, Jack, and Peter Ackerman. *A Force More Powerful: A Century of Nonviolent Conflict*. New York: Palgrave Macmillan Limited, 2001.

Edinger, Edward. *Archetype of the Apocalypse: A Jungian Study of the Book of Revelation*. Ed. George R. Elder. Chicago: Open Court Company, 1999.

Eisler, Riane. *The Chalice and the Blade : Our History, Our Future*. San Francisco: Harper & Row, 1988.

Ferreira, Eleonora C., and Joao P. Ferreira. *Making Sense of the Media : A Handbook of Popular Education Techniques*. New York: Monthly Review Press, 1996.

Fillingham, Lydia A., and Moshe Susser. *Foucault for Beginners*. Danbury, CT: For Beginners, 2007.

A Force More Powerful. Dir. Steve York. DVD. 2000.

Foucault, Michel. *The Foucault Reader*. Ed. Paul Rabinow. New York: Pantheon, 1988.

Frank, Thomas. *The Conquest of Cool: Business Culture, Counterculture, and the Rise of Hip Consumerism*. Chicago: University of Chicago Press, 1997.

Frank, Thomas. *What's the Matter with Kansas?: How Conservatives Won the Heart of America*. New York: Owl Books, 2005.

Freire, Paulo. *Pedagogy of Hope: Reliving Pedagogy of the Oppressed*. London: Burns & Oates, 1997.

——. *Pedagogy of the Oppressed*. New York: Continuum, 1997.

Gelobter, Michel, Michael Dorsey, Leslie Fields, Tom Goldtooth, Anuja Mendiratta, Richard Moore, Rachel Morello-Frosch, Peggy M. Shepard, and Gerald Torres. *The Soul of Environmentalism: Rediscovering Transformational Politics in the 21st Century*. http://www.rprogress.org/soul/soul.pdf

Giroux, Henry A., Colin Lankshear, and Michael Peters. *Counternarratives*. New York: Routledge, 1996.

——. *Public Spaces, Private Lives: Beyond the Culture of Cynicism*. Lanham: Rowman & Littlefield, Incorporated, 2001.

Gitlin, Todd. *The Sixties: Years of Hope, Days of Rage*. New York: Broadway Books, 1993.

Gladwell, Malcolm. *Blink: The Power of Thinking Without Thinking.* New York: Back Bay, 2007.

——. *The Tipping Point: How Little Things Can Make a Big Difference.* New York: Back Bay, 2002.

Goffman, Erving. *Frame Analysis.* New York: Harper Colophon, 1974.

Gore, Al. *An Inconvenient Truth: The Planetary Emergency of Global Warming and What We Can Do about It.* Emmaus, PA: Rodale Press, Incorporated, 2006.

Gottlieb, Robert. *Forcing the Spring: The Transformation of the American Environmental Movement.* Washington, DC: Island Press, 2005.

Gramsci, Antonio. *The Antonio Gramsci Reader: Selected Writings, 1916-1935.* Ed. David Forgacs and Eric J. Hobsbawm. New York: New York University Press, 2000.

Hardisty, Jean, and Wilma P. Mankiller. *Mobilizing Resentment: Conservative Resurgence from the John Birch Society to the Promise Keepers.* New York: Beacon Press, 2000.

Hardt, Michael, and Antonio Negri. *Empire.* New York: Harvard University Press, 2001.

——. *Multitude: War and Democracy in the Age of Empire.* New York: Penguin Press HC, 2004.

Hartman, Harry. *Marketing in the Soul Age: Building Lifestyle Worlds.* New York: Hartman Group, 2001.

Heath, Chip, and Dan Heath. *Made to Stick: Why Some Ideas Survive and Others Die.* New York: Random House, 2007.

Herman, Edward S., and Noam Chomsky. *Manufacturing Consent: The Political Economy of the Mass Media.* New York: Pantheon, 1988.

Hernandez, Adriana. *Pedagogy, Democracy, and Feminism: Rethinking the Public Sphere.* New York: State University of New York Press, 1997.

Hoffer, Eric. *The True Believer: Thoughts on the Nature of Mass Movements.* New York: HarperCollins, 1989.

Holloway, John. *Change the World Without Taking Power: The Meaning of Revolution Today.* London: Pluto Press, 2005.

hooks, bell. *Feminism Is for Everybody : Passionate Politics.* Cambridge, MA: South End Press, 2000.

——. *Feminist Theory: From Margin to Center.* Ed. Manning Marable. Cambridge, MA: South End Press, 2000.

Horton, Myles, and Paulo Freire. *We Make the Road by Walking: Conversations on Education and Social Change*. Ed. Brenda Bell. Philadelphia: Temple University Press, 1990.

Horton, Myles, Judith Kohl, and Herbert R. Kohl. *The Long Haul: An Autobiography*. New York: Teachers College Press, Teachers College, Columbia University, 1998.

Horwitz, Claudia. *The Spiritual Activist: Practices to Transform Your Life, Your Work, and Your World*. New York: Penguin, 2002.

Howe, Neil, William Strauss, and R. J. Matson. *Millenials Rising: The Next Great Generation*. New York: Vintage, 2000.

Huxley, Aldous. *Brave New World*. New York: Harper and Row, 1932.

Hyde, Lewis. *The Gift: Creativity and the Artist in the Modern World*. New York: Vintage, 2007.

——. *Trickster Makes This World: Mischief, Myth, and Art*. New York: Canongate Books, 2008.

Jasper, James M. *The Art of Moral Protest: Culture, Biography, and Creativity in Social Movements*. Chicago: University of Chicago Press, 1998.

Joseph, Peniel E. *Waiting 'Til the Midnight Hour: A Narrative History of Black Power in America*. New York: Owl Books, 2007.

Kahn, Si. *Organizing: A Guide for Grassroots Leaders*. New York: N A S W P, 1991.

Kaufman, Cynthia. *Ideas for Action: Relevant Theory for Radical Change*. Cambridge, MA: South End Press, 2003.

King, Martin Luther, Jr. *A Testament of Hope: The Essential Writings and Speeches of Martin Luther King, Jr.* Ed. James M. Washington. Grand Rapids, MI: Zondervan, 1991.

Kivel, Paul, and Howard Zinn. *Uprooting Racism: How White People Can Work for Racial Justice*. Gabriola Island, BC: New Society Publishers, Limited, 2002.

Klein, Naomi. *No Logo: Taking Aim at the Brand Bullies*. New York: Picador, 2000.

——. *The Shock Doctrine: The Rise of Disaster Capitalism*. New York: Metropolitan Books, 2007.

Korten, David C. *The Great Turning: From Empire to Earth Community*. San Francisco: Berrett-Koehler, Incorporated, 2007.

——. *The Post-Corporate World: Life after Capitalism.* San Francisco: Berrett-Koehler, Incorporated, 1999.

Lakey, George. *Strategy for a Living Revolution.* Grossman, 1973.

Lakoff, George. *Moral Politics : How Liberals and Conservatives Think.* Chicago: University of Chicago Press, 2002.

——. *Thinking Points: Communicating Our American Values and Vision: A Progressive's Handbook.* New York: Farrar, Straus & Giroux, 2006.

——. *Whose Freedom?: The Battle over America's Most Important Idea.* New York: Picador, 2007.

Lasn, Kalle. *Culture Jam: The Uncooling of America.* New York: Harper-Collins, 1999.

Lee. Martha F. *Earth First! Environmental Apocalypse.* Syracuse, NY: Syracuse University Press, 1995.

Leiss, William, Stephen Kline, and Sut Jhally. *Social Communication in Advertising: Persons, Products and Images of Well-Being.* New York: Methuen & Company, Limited, 1986.

Light, Andrew, ed. *Social Ecology after Bookchin.* New York: Guilford Publications, Incorporated, 1998.

Lohmann, Larry, ed. *Carbon Trading: A Critical Conversation on Climate Change, Privatization, and Power.* Uppsala, Sweden: Development Dialogue/Corner House/Dag Hammarskjold Foundation, 2006.

Lorde, Audre. *Sister Outsider: Essays and Speeches.* Berkeley CA: Crossing Press, 2007.

Lui, Meizhu, Barbara Robles, and Betsy Leondar-Wright. *The Color of Wealth: The Story Behind the U. S. Racial Wealth Divide.* New York: New Press, 2006.

Luntz, Frank. *Words That Work: It's Not What You Say, It's What People Hear.* New York: Hyperion Press, 2007.

Lynch, Aaron. *Thought Contagion: How Belief Spreads Through Society.* New York: Basic Books, 1996.

Malkan, Stacy. *Not Just a Pretty Face: The Ugly Side of the Beauty Industry.* Gabriola Island, BC: New Society, Limited, 2007.

Mander, Mary S., ed. *Framing Friction: Media and Social Conflict.* Urbana, IL: University of Illinois Press, 1998.

Marcos, Subcomandante I. *Our Word Is Our Weapon: Selected Writings of Subcomandante Marcos.* Ed. Juana Ponce de Leon. New York: Seven Stories Press, 2004.

Martinez, Elizabeth, and Angela Y. Davis. *De Colores Means All of Us: Latina Views for a Multi-Colored Century*. Cambridge MA: South End Press, 1998.

Marx, Karl, and Friedrich Engels. *The Communist Manifesto*. Ed. Gareth S. Jones. New York: Penguin Group (USA) Incorporated, 2002.

McKenzie-Mohr, Doug, and William Smith. *Fostering Sustainable Behavior: An Introduction to Community-Based Social Marketing*. Gabriola Island, BC: New Society, Limited, 2000.

McLuhan, Eric, Frank Zingrone, and Marshall McLuhan, eds. *The Essential McLuhan*. New York: Basic Books, 1996.

McMurtry, John. *The Cancer Stage of Capitalism*. New York: Pluto Press, 1998.

Minch, Holly, ed. *Loud & Clear in an Election Year: Amplifying the Voices of Community Advocates*. San Francisco: SPIN Project, 2004.

Mitchell, Don. *The Right to the City: Social Justice and the Fight for Public Space*. Minneapolis: Guilford Publications, Incorporated, 2003.

Moore Lappe, Frances. *Getting a Grip: Clarity, Creativity, and Courage in a World Gone Mad*. North Mankato: Small Planet Media, 2007.

Moraga, Cherríe, and Anzaldúa, Gloria, Ed. *This Bridge Called My Back: Writings by Radical Women of Color*. New York: Kitchen Table Women of Color Press, 1983.

Moyer, Bill. *Doing Democracy: The MAP Model for Organizing Social Movements*. Gabriola Island, BC: New Society, Limited, 2001.

Mumby, Dennis K., ed. *Narrative and Social Control: Critical Perspectives*. Newbury Park, CA: SAGE Publications, Incorporated, 1993.

Notes from Nowhere Collective *We Are Everywhere: The Irresistible Rise of Global Anti Capitalism*. New York: Verso Books, 2003.

Nunberg, Geoff. *Talking Right: How Conservatives Turned Liberalism into a Tax-Raising, Latte-Drinking, Sushi-Eating, Volvo-Driving, New York Times-Reading, Body-Piercing, Hollywood-Loving, Left-Wing Freak Show*. New York: Public Affairs, 2006.

Orwell, George. *1984*. New York: Signet Classic, 1949.

Popcorn, Faith, and Adam Hanft. *The Dictionary of the Future: The Words, Terms and Trends that Define the Way We'll Live, Work and Talk*. New York: Hyperion Press, 2001.

Parry, Alan, and Robert E. Doan. *Story Re-Visions: Narrative Therapy in the Postmodern World*. New York: Guilford Press, 1994.

Payne, Charles M. *I've Got the Light of Freedom: The Organizing Tradition and the Mississippi Freedom Struggle*. Berkeley, CA: University of California Press, 2007.

Penn, Mark. *Microtrends: The Small Forces Behind Tomorrow's Big Changes*. New York: Twelve, 2007.

The Persuaders. Dir. Barak Goodman and Rachel Dretzin. DVD. 2003.

Polletta, Francesca. *It Was Like a Fever: Storytelling in Protest and Politics*. Chicago: University of Chicago Press, 2006.

Powell, Jim, and Joe Lee. *Postmodernism for Beginners*. Danbury, CT: For Beginners, 2007.

The Power of Nightmares. Dir. Adam Curtis. DVD. 2007.

Rampton, Sheldon, and John Stauber. *Trust Us, We're Experts!: How Industry Manipulates Science and Gambles with Your Future*. New York: Tarcher, 2002.

———. *Weapons of Mass Deception: The Uses of Propaganda in Bush's War on Iraq*. New York: Jeremy P. Tarcher Incorporated, 2003.

Ray, Paul H., and Sherry R. Anderson. *The Cultural Creatives : How 50 Million People Are Changing the World*. New York: Three Rivers Press, 2001.

Ray, Paul H. *A New Values Survey, on the Emerging Wisdom Culture and New Political Compass*. Unpublished monograph, 2008.

Reclaiming Revolution: history, summation, and lessons from Standing Together to Organize a Revolutionary Movement (STORM). Oakland, CA: STORM, 2003.

Roberts, Kevin. *Lovemarks: The Future Beyond Brands*. New York: PowerHouse Books, 2005.

Rubin, Jerry. *Do It!* New York: Simon and Schuster, 1970.

Rushkoff, Douglas. *Media Virus! Hidden Agendas in Popular Culture*. New York: Random House, 1994.

Ryan, Charlotte. *Prime Time Activism: Media Strategies for Grassroots Organizing*. Cambridge, MA: South End Press, 1991.

Sharp, Gene, Joshua Paulson, and Christopher Miller. *Waging Nonviolent Struggle: 20th Century Practice and 21st Century Potential*. New York: Porter Sargent, Incorporated, 2005.

———. *Power and Struggle: Part One of the Politics of Nonviolent Action*. Ed. Marina Finkelstein. Boston: Porter Sargent, Incorporated, 1973.

———. *The Dynamics of Nonviolent Action: Part Three of the Politics of Nonviolent Action*. Ed. Marina Finkelstein. Boston: Porter Sargent, Incorporated, 1973.

Sharp, Gene. *The Politics of Nonviolent Action Part Two: The Methods of Nonviolent Action*. Ed. Marina Finkelstein. Boston: Porter Sargent, Incorporated, 1973.

Shields, Katrina. *In the Tiger's Mouth: An Empowerment Guide for Social Action*. Gabriola Island, BC: New Society Publishers, Limited, 1994.

Shepard, Benjamin, and Ronald Hayduck, eds. *From ACT up to the WTO: Urban Protest and Community Building in the Era of Globalization*. New York: Verso Books, 2002.

Shirky, Clay. *Here Comes Everybody: The Power of Organization Without Organizations*. New York: Penguin Press, 2008.

Shukaitis, Stevphen and David Graeber Eds.*Constituent Imagination: Militant Investigation, Collective Theorization*. Oakland, CA: AK Press, 2007.

Smith, Paul C., and Robert A. Warrior. *Like a Hurricane: The Indian Movement from Alcatraz to Wounded Knee*. New York: New Press, 1996.

Solnit, David B., ed. *Globalize Liberation: How to Uproot the System and Build a Better World*. San Francisco: City Lights Books, 2003.

Stauber, John, Sheldon Rampton, and Mark Dowie. *Toxic Sludge Is Good for You!: Lies, Damn Lies and the Public Relations Industry*. Monroe, ME: Common Courage Press, 1995.

Storey, John. *Inventing Popular Culture: From Folklore to Globalization*. Malden, MA: Blackwell Limited, 2008.

Szanto, Andre, ed. *What Orwell Didn't Know: Propaganda and the New Face of American Politics*. New York: Public Affairs, 2007.

Takaki, Ronald T. *A Different Mirror: A History of Multicultural America*. New York: Back Bay, 1994.

Taleb, Nassim N. *The Black Swan: The Impact of the Highly Improbable*. New York: Random House, 2007.

Tarrow, Sidney, Robert H. Bates, and Ellen Comisso. *Power in Movement : Social Movements and Contentious Politics*. Cambridge [England] ; New York: Cambridge University Press, 1998.

Tong, Rosemarie. *Feminist Thought : A More Comprehensive Introduction*. Boulder, CO: Westview Press, 1989.

Re:Imagining Change

Tzu, Sun. *The Art of War.* Trans. Thomas Cleary. Minneapolis: Shambhala Publications, Incorporated, 1989.

Wallack, Lawrence, Lori Dorfman, David Jernigan, and Makani Themba. *Media Advocacy and Public Health: Power for Prevention.* Newbury Park, CA: SAGE Publications, Incorporated, 1993.

Weiler, Kathleen, Henry A. Giroux, and Paulo Freire. *Women Teaching for Change: Gender, Class and Power.* South Hadley, MA: Bergin & Garvey, 1987.

Westen, Drew. *The Political Brain: The Role of Emotion in Deciding the Fate of the Nation.* New York: Public Affairs, 2007.

Weyle, Rex. *Greenpeace: How A Group of Ecologists, Journalists, and Visionaries Changed The World.* Emmaus, PA: Rodale International Ltd.

Woman of Color Against Violence, INCITE!, ed. *The Revolution Will Not Be Funded: Beyond the Non-Profit Industrial Complex.* Cambridge, MA: South End Press, 2007.

Yes Men, The. *The Yes Men: The True Story of the End of the World Trade Organization.* Boston: Disinformation Company Limited, 2004.

Zerubavel, Eviatar. *The Elephant in the Room: Silence and Denial in Everyday Life.* Oxford [England] ; New York: Oxford University Press, Incorporated, 2007.

Zimbardo, Philip G. *The Lucifer Effect: Understanding How Good People Turn Evil.* New York: Random House, 2007.

Zinn, Howard. *A People's History of the United States.* New York: Harper Perennial, 1980.

About *Smart*Meme

*Smart*Meme's mission is to build movements and amplify the impact of grassroots organizing with new strategy and training resources, values-based communications, collaborations, and meme campaigning. *Smart*Meme uses the power of narrative to advance a holistic vision of grassroots social change that connects struggles for democracy, peace, justice, and ecological sanity.

*Smart*Meme supports social change initiatives by offering tools, training, and strategy development. We connect leaders to develop shared stories and common visions for change, and collaborate with a diverse range of organizational partners. *Smart*Meme innovates practices in the sector through experimentation, research and development, and creative cultural intervention. We have worked behind the scenes in scores of campaigns, demonstrations and mass direct actions, from protests against the 2003 Free Trade Area of the Americas Summit in Miami to supporting Iraq and Afghanistan veterans telling their stories at Winter Soldier, to amplifying the voices of Indigenous leaders and community organizers marching out of the 2009 Copenhagen Climate talks.

We believe that fundamental social change is not only possible but urgently needed, and that people-powered grassroots social movements, led by people who are most directly affected, are the engines of true social progress.

*Smart*Meme has trained over 3,000 activists and collaborated with over 100 organizations since 2002. We have found that story is a powerful tool to reach across issues, connect generations, and bridge the fault lines of race, gender, and class. We have applied story-based strategy in a range of different contexts: from youth-veteran collaborations to end the war in Iraq, to challenging the destructive practices of multinational corporations, to efforts to promote the Precautionary Principle as a policy tool for environmental justice.

We believe that fundamental social change is not only possible but urgently needed, and that people-powered grassroots social movements, led by people who are most directly affected, are the engines of true social progress. We are cultivating a thriving community of innovative practitioners who are changing the story and changing the world. Visit us online and get involved at www.smartmeme.org

About the Authors

Doyle Canning is a strategist, trainer, and organizer with a deep commitment to building 21st century social movements for ecological justice. She came to the smartMeme collective in 2003 after studying critical pedagogy, working as a grassroots organizer, and being banned from Australia for her rabble rousing. As co-director at *smart*Meme, Doyle serves social movements a facilitator, message maker, campaign consultant, and coach. She is a contributor to *Letters from Young Activists* (Nation Books, 2005), and has served on the advisory funding panel of the Haymarket People's Fund, an antiracist social change foundation. Doyle practices yoga, sings from the heart, reveres nature, and celebrates life. She lives in Boston, Massachusetts.

Patrick Reinsborough has been involved in campaigns for peace, the environment, democracy, indigenous rights and economic justice for over twenty years. He previously served as the Organizing Director of the Rainforest Action Network where he helped organize mass nonviolent direct actions to shut down the Seattle meeting of the World Trade Organization and the April 2000 meetings of the World Bank and International Monetary Fund. In 2002 he co-founded the *smart*Meme strategy & training project as a vehicle to explore the intersections of social change strategy, imagination and narrative. Several of his earlier strategy essays are published in *Globalize Liberation: How to Uproot the System and Build a Better World* (City Lights Press 2004) Patrick spends his time parenting, playing music for his friends, and wandering through the urban wilds of San Francisco.

ABOUT PM PRESS

PM Press was founded at the end of 2007 by a small collection of folks with decades of publishing, media, and organizing experience. PM co-founder Ramsey Kanaan started AK Press as a young teenager in Scotland almost 30 years ago and, together with his fellow PM Press co-conspirators, has published and distributed hundreds of books, pamphlets, CDs, and DVDs. Members of PM have founded enduring book fairs, spearheaded victorious tenant organizing campaigns, and worked closely with bookstores, academic conferences, and even rock bands to deliver political and challenging ideas to all walks of life. We're old enough to know what we're doing and young enough to know what's at stake.

We seek to create radical and stimulating fiction and non-fiction books, pamphlets, t-shirts, visual and audio materials to entertain, educate and inspire you. We aim to distribute these through every available channel with every available technology - whether that means you are seeing anarchist classics at our bookfair stalls; reading our latest vegan cookbook at the café; downloading geeky fiction e-books; or digging new music and timely videos from our website.

PM Press is always on the lookout for talented and skilled volunteers, artists, activists and writers to work with. If you have a great idea for a project or can contribute in some way, please get in touch.

PM Press
PO Box 23912
Oakland, CA 94623
www.pmpress.org

FRIENDS OF PM PRESS

These are indisputably momentous times – the financial system is melting down globally and the Empire is stumbling. Now more than ever there is a vital need for radical ideas.

In the year since its founding – and on a mere shoestring – PM Press has risen to the formidable challenge of publishing and distributing knowledge and entertainment for the struggles ahead. With over 75 releases to date, we have published an impressive and stimulating array of literature, art, music, politics, and culture. Using every available medium, we've succeeded in connecting those hungry for ideas and information to those putting them into practice.

Friends of PM allows you to directly help impact, amplify, and revitalize the discourse and actions of radical writers, filmmakers, and artists. It provides us with a stable foundation from which we can build upon our early successes and provides a much-needed subsidy for the materials that can't necessarily pay their own way. You can help make that happen – and receive every new title automatically delivered to your door once a month – by joining as a Friend of PM Press. Here are your options:

- **$25 a month** Get all books and pamphlets plus 50% discount on all webstore purchases
- **$25 a month** Get all CDs and DVDs plus 50% discount on all webstore purchases
- **$40 a month** Get all PM Press releases plus 50% discount on all webstore purchases
- **$100 a month** Sustainer – Everything plus PM merchandise, free downloads, and 50% discount on all webstore purchases

Your Visa or Mastercard will be billed once a month, until you tell us to stop. Or until our efforts succeed in bringing the revolution around. Or the financial meltdown of Capital makes plastic redundant. Whichever comes first.

In and Out of Crisis: The Global Financial Meltdown and Left Alternatives

Greg Albo, Sam Gindin, Leo Panitch

978-1-60486-212-6
160 pages
$13.95

While many around the globe are increasingly wondering if another world is indeed possible, few are mapping out potential avenues – and flagging wrong turns – en route to a post-capitalist future. In this groundbreaking analysis of the financial meltdown, renowned radical political economists Albo, Gindin and Panitch lay bare the roots of the crisis in the inner logic of capitalism itself.

With an unparalleled understanding of capitalism, the authors provocatively challenge the call by much of the Left for a return to a largely mythical Golden Age of economic regulation as a check on finance capital unbound. They deftly illuminate how the era of neoliberal free markets has been, in practice, under-girded by state intervention on a massive scale. The authors argue that it's time to start thinking about genuinely transformative alternatives to capitalism – and how to build the collective capacity to get us there. *In and Out of Crisis* stands to be the enduring critique of the crisis and an indispensable springboard for a renewed Left.

"Greg Albo, Sam Gindin, and Leo Panitch provide a perceptive, and persuasive, analysis of the origins of the crisis, arguing that the left must go beyond the demand for re-regulation, which, they assert, will not solve the economic or environmental crisis, and must instead demand public control of the banks and the financial sector, and of the uses to which finance is put. This is an important book that should be read widely, especially by those hoping to revitalize the left."
— Barbara Epstein, author of *The Minsk Ghetto 1941–1943: Jewish Resistance and Soviet Internationalism*

"The Left has often been accused of not understanding economics properly. So it's been no small pleasure over the last year to see the guardians of neo-liberal orthodoxy thrashing around helplessly in a bid to explain the financial meltdown... Leo Panitch has stood out in recent years as one of the socialist intellectuals most fully engaged with political questions, analyzing the problems faced by left-wing parties, trade unions and other social movements with great clarity."
— *Irish Left Review*

Re:Imagining Change

Capital and Its Discontents: Conversations with Radical Thinkers in a Time of Tumult

Sasha Lilley

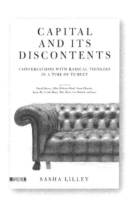

978-1-60486-334-5
320 pages
$20.00

Capitalism is stumbling, empire is faltering, and the planet is thawing. Yet many people are still grasping to understand these multiple crises and to find a way forward to a just future. Into the breach come the essential insights of *Capital and Its Discontents*, which cut through the gristle to get to the heart of the matter about the nature of capitalism and its inner workings. Through a series of incisive conversations with some of the most eminent thinkers and political economists on the Left – including David Harvey, Ellen Meiksins Wood, Mike Davis, Leo Panitch, Tariq Ali, and Noam Chomsky – *Capital and Its Discontents* illuminates the dynamic contradictions undergirding capitalism and the potential for its dethroning. At a moment when capitalism as a system is more reviled than ever, here is an indispensable toolbox of ideas for action by some of the most brilliant thinkers of our times.

"These conversations illuminate the current world situation in ways that are very useful for those hoping to orient themselves and find a way forward to effective individual and collective action. Highly recommended."
— Kim Stanley Robinson, *New York Times* bestselling author of the *Mars* Trilogy and *The Years of Rice and Salt*

"This is an extremely important book. It is the most detailed, comprehensive, and best study yet published on the most recent capitalist crisis and its discontents. Sasha Lilley sets each interview in its context, writing with style, scholarship and wit about ideas and philosophies."
— Andrej Grubacic, radical sociologist and social critic, co-author of *Wobblies and Zapatistas*

"In this fine set of interviews, an A-list of radical political economists demonstrate why their skills are indispensable to understanding today's multiple economic and ecological crises."
— Raj Patel, author of *Stuffed and Starved* and *The Value of Nothing*

Global Slump:
The Economics and Politics
of Crisis and Resistance
David McNally

978-1-60486-332-1
176 pages
$15.95

Global Slump analyzes the world financial
meltdown as the first *systemic* crisis of the
neoliberal stage of capitalism. It argues that – far
from having ended – the crisis has ushered in a
whole period of worldwide economic and political turbulence. In developing
an account of the crisis as rooted in fundamental features of capitalism,
Global Slump challenges the view that its source lies in financial deregulation.
It offers an original account of the "financialization" of the world economy
and explores the connections between international financial markets and
new forms of debt and dispossession, particularly in the Global South.
The book shows that, while averting a complete meltdown, the massive
intervention by central banks laid the basis for recurring crises for poor and
working class people. It traces new patterns of social resistance for building
an anti-capitalist opposition to the damage that neoliberal capitalism is
inflicting on the lives of millions.

*"In this book, McNally confirms – once again – his standing as one of the world's
leading Marxist scholars of capitalism. For a scholarly, in depth analysis of our
current crisis that never loses sight of its political implications (for them and for us),
expressed in a language that leaves no reader behind, there is simply no better place
to go."*
— Bertell Ollman, Professor, Department of Politics, NYU, and author of *Dance of
the Dialectic: Steps in Marx's Method*

*"David McNally's tremendously timely book is packed with significant theoretical
and practical insights, and offers actually-existing examples of what is to be done.*
Global Slump *urgently details how changes in the capitalist space-economy over
the past 25 years, especially in the forms that money takes, have expanded wide-
scale vulnerabilities for all kinds of people, and how people fight back. In a word,
the problem isn't neo-liberalism – it's capitalism."*
— Ruth Wilson Gilmore, University of Southern California and author, *Golden Gulag*

142

Notes

Notes